# TELL ME ABOUT YOURSELF

## JOB INTERVIEWS

### 101 WAYS TO NAIL THE INTERVIEW AND GET THE OFFER

## SHANNON MICHELLE

# CONTENTS

# INTRODUCTION

 *Opportunities don't happen; you create them.*

— CHRIS GROSSER

This is not just another book on acing interviews; it is a game-changer, a confidence-booster, and a career-enhancer all rolled into one. If you have ever felt the dread and anxiety that comes with facing interviews, if you have ever stumbled over your words when asked that seemingly simple question, or if you have grappled with the frustration of not knowing how to stand out in a crowded job market, then this book is exactly what you have been looking for.

We have all been there—sitting across the table from a potential employer, feeling the weight of their expectations, and trying to conjure up the perfect response to "Tell me about yourself." It is a nerve-wracking experience that can leave even the most seasoned professionals feeling like a deer in headlights. The struggle is real, and you're not alone in feeling the pressure to perform to the best of your abilities.

In today's ultra-competitive job market, landing the perfect job has become more challenging than ever. With technological advancements, automation, and global connectivity, the odds are stacked against you (Semuels, 2023). It is no wonder that the mere thought of an interview can send shivers down your spine. Don't worry; I am here to provide you with the tools, strategies, and confidence you need to navigate this daunting landscape with ease.

So, why did you decide to invest in this book? Perhaps it was the constant string of rejections despite your best efforts. Maybe it was the overwhelming sense of frustration at not being able to effectively communicate your value to potential employers. Or it could be the burning desire to finally take control of your career path and land that dream job. Whatever your catalyst may have been, I assure you that you have made the right choice.

With this book, you will gain access to invaluable shortcuts that will fast-track your success. You will uncover the secrets to crafting a compelling narrative, honing your personal brand, and navigating the interview process with finesse. I will also speak about the IMPRESS framework. This framework is not just a set of guidelines; it is a roadmap to success in the world of interviews. So, what is it about?

- **I—Immerse Yourself in the Intel:** Before walking into an interview, it is essential to arm yourself with knowledge about the company, the role you are applying for, and the industry as a whole.

- **M—Market Yourself:** Just like any successful brand, you need to market yourself effectively during an interview. Showcase your unique selling points, highlight your accomplishments, and convey the value you bring to the table.
- **P—Prep Like a Pro:** Preparation is the key to success in any interview scenario. From practicing common interview questions to fine-tuning your responses, diligent preparation gives you the edge you need to excel.
- **R—Resonate With Realness:** Authenticity is a powerful tool that makes a lasting impact during an interview. Embrace your true self, share genuine stories and experiences, and connect with your interviewers on a personal level.
- **E—Engage Through Your Delivery:** Communication is key in any interview setting. Focus on delivering your responses clearly, confidently, and with conviction.
- **S—Stand Out in Every Format:** In today's digital age, interviews come in various formats, from in-person meetings to virtual sessions. To stand out from the crowd, adapt your approach to suit each format.
- **S—Seal the Deal:** The final step in the IMPRESS framework is all about sealing the deal. Follow up after the interview with a thank-you note, reiterating your interest in the role and expressing gratitude for the opportunity.

And the results speak for themselves. Picture this: walking into an interview room radiating confidence, captivating the interviewers with your authenticity, and leaving an indelible impression that secures you the job offer. This is not just a fantasy; it is your future after reading this book.

## WHO AM I?

I am not just another voice in the crowd. I am Shannon Michelle, a seasoned professional and a trusted guide. I have the ability to help individuals like you transform your interview experiences. My authority and expertise in this field make me uniquely qualified to be your mentor on this journey toward interview mastery.

I have had the privilege to sit across from prospective employers, experiencing the nervous anticipation that comes with being in the hot seat. I have also been on the receiving end of panel interviews and, at one point, found myself facing a conference table of potential coworkers, each firing off their individual questions. Post-COVID, remote interviews became the new battleground for entry to the workplace. Knowing your audience and how you are received is that much more difficult over video conference.

My multifaceted experiences have given me valuable insights into the intricacies of the interview process in various settings, including the unique challenges associated with the shift to remote interviews. These experiences have shaped my approach and understanding of the interview landscape, allowing me to tailor my guidance to meet the evolving needs of today's interviewees.

As you embark on this transformative journey, you will come to realize that this is not just any book—it is the *right* book for you. It is the beacon of hope, the gateway to your triumphs, and the compass that will guide you toward the career of your dreams. So, buckle up, dive in, and get ready to conquer the interview room with this book as your trusted companion.

# 1

# ❶—IMMERSE YOURSELF IN THE INTEL

> *By failing to prepare, you are preparing to fail.*
>
> — BENJAMIN FRANKLIN

L et's begin by exploring the world of job interviews and unlock the secrets to ace them like a pro. In this chapter, I'm going to equip you with the essential tools and strategies to immerse yourself and skyrocket your confidence for that next big interview.

Let's kick things off with a mind-blowing statistic that sheds light on the importance of researching the company before your interview: 47% of recruiters have admitted that they would reject a candidate who lacks knowledge about the company they are applying to (*8 Surprising Statistics About Interviews*, n.d.). That is almost half!

The first crucial step in mastering the art of interviews is to understand the hiring process and the job description inside out. Why? By getting into the nitty-gritty details of the job requirements and decoding what the employer is really looking for, you can position yourself as the perfect fit for the role and demonstrate how your skills align seamlessly with the company's needs.

Imagine walking into the interview room armed with a thorough understanding of what the job entails, the company culture, and the specific qualities the hiring manager is seeking. You will not only exude confidence and professionalism but also showcase your genuine interest in the role, which can set you apart from the sea of other candidates.

## 1. LOOK AT THE BIG PICTURE

Let's begin by looking at the overall hiring process (*The Hiring Process Explained in 15 Steps*, n.d.). When you are feeling nervous about interviews, understanding the overall hiring process can provide much-needed clarity and a sense of control.

- Application Review: The process typically begins with an employer posting a job opening and receiving applications from interested candidates.
- Initial Screening: Candidates who make the cut in the initial review may undergo an initial screening, which could involve a phone interview or an online assessment.
- Interviews: The next phase often includes one or more interviews conducted by various stakeholders, such as HR representatives, hiring managers, or potential team members.

- Assessment and Testing: Depending on the role, candidates may be asked to complete job-specific assessments or tests to evaluate their technical abilities, problem-solving skills, or behavioral competencies.
- Reference and Background Checks: Following the interviews and assessments, employers may reach out to the candidate's provided references to gather insights into their work ethic, performance, and character.
- Job Offer: Finally, the selected candidate receives a formal job offer outlining the terms of employment, including compensation, benefits, and start date.

## 2. DECODE THE JOB DESCRIPTION

When dealing with interview jitters, deciphering a job description can be a game-changer (Mays, 2025). Here's what you should look out for:

### Understanding Job Titles

When evaluating job titles, it is important to look beyond the superficial title itself and focus on the actual responsibilities and qualifications associated with the position. To ensure alignment between the job title and your skills and experience, consider the following steps:

- Analyze Job Descriptions: Carefully read the job description to understand the key responsibilities, duties, and qualifications required for the role.

- Compare Your Skills: Evaluate your own skills and experiences in relation to the requirements outlined in the job description.
- Understand Career Goals: Consider how the job aligns with your long-term career goals. Assess whether the position offers opportunities for growth, learning, and advancement in your desired field.
- Seek Clarifications: If the job title or responsibilities are unclear, don't hesitate to contact the hiring manager or HR representative for more information.
- Research Industry Norms: In some industries, job titles can be more standardized, while in others, they may vary widely. Research typical job titles and roles within your industry to gain a better perspective on how your skills and experiences align with the position.

### Key Responsibilities and Duties

When reviewing the key responsibilities and duties outlined in a job description, it is essential to thoroughly identify the core tasks that the role entails. Here are a few steps to help you understand and align with the responsibilities:

- Core Responsibilities: Begin by identifying the primary responsibilities that are crucial to the role. These are often listed at the beginning of the job description and provide an overview of what the position entails.
- Duties and Tasks: Dive deeper into the specific duties and tasks expected in the role. These details

can provide insight into the day-to-day activities you will be engaged in if you are hired.

- Strengths and Expertise: Highlight any tasks that directly resonate with your strengths and expertise. Focus on areas where you have excelled in the past and can leverage your skills to excel in the new role.
- Skill Showcasing Opportunities: Look for opportunities within the job description where you can showcase your skills and expertise. Pay attention to tasks that allow you to make a meaningful impact within the role and contribute positively to the organization.
- Value Addition: Identify ways you can add value beyond the basic job requirements. Consider how you can go above and beyond in fulfilling the responsibilities and duties outlined in the job description.

### *Required Qualifications*

When reviewing the required qualifications listed in a job description, it is crucial to assess how your own qualifications align with the specified requirements. Here is an overview of how to approach this task effectively:

- Educational Requirements: Pay attention to any specific educational qualifications mentioned in the job description, such as a degree, certification, or relevant coursework.
- Certifications and Licenses: Note any certifications, licenses, or professional credentials that are required for the position. If you possess these qualifications,

make sure to highlight them in your application to demonstrate your readiness for the role.

- Specific Skills and Experiences: Look for specific skills, experiences, or competencies that are crucial for the role. Assess how your own skills and experiences align with these requirements.
- Alignment with Requirements: Evaluate the degree to which your qualifications align with the listed requirements.
- Transferable Skills: Consider any transferable skills you have acquired from previous roles or experiences that may apply to the position.
- Professional Development: If there are gaps in your qualifications, identify opportunities for professional development or upskilling to bridge those gaps.

### Desired Skills and Competencies

When reviewing the desired skills and competencies outlined in a job description, it is crucial to carefully examine the employer's wish list and consider how your own skills align with the desired qualifications. Here is how to effectively address this task:

- Critical Analysis: Begin by thoroughly evaluating the desired skills and competencies listed in the job description.
- Overlap with Your Skills: Identify any overlap between the desired skills and competencies and your own skill set.
- Relevant Experiences: Highlight professional experiences or specific achievements that

demonstrate your proficiency in the desired skills and competencies.

- Adaptability and Learning Agility: Even if you do not possess every single desired skill and competency, emphasize your adaptability and learning agility.
- Value Proposition: Express how your skills and competencies can add value to the organization. Clearly communicate how your unique strengths align with the desired qualifications and how they can contribute to the success of the team and the company as a whole.
- Professional Development Plan: If there are gaps between the desired skills and your current skill set, present a professional development plan.

### Company Culture and Values

When evaluating the company culture, mission, and values outlined in a job description, it is essential to carefully consider how your professional values and work style align with those of the organization. Here is how to assess a company's values:

- Assess the Company's Culture and Values: Start by thoroughly examining the information provided in the job description about the company's culture, mission, and values.
- Reflect on Your Professional Values and Work Style: Consider the type of work environment in which you thrive, your preferred communication and collaboration styles, and the values that are important to you in a workplace setting.

- Alignments and Overlaps: Identify any alignments or overlaps between the company's stated culture and values and your professional beliefs and work style.
- Cultural Fit Demonstration: Provide specific examples that demonstrate your ability to thrive in environments that align with the company's culture and values.
- Cultural Contribution: Articulate how your values and work style can contribute to and enhance the company's culture.
- Openness and Adaptability: Express your openness to embracing the company's culture and values while also highlighting your adaptability.

## 3. RESEARCH THE COMPANY

Mastering the interview process involves thorough research on the company (*How to Research a Company for a Job Interview*, 2021). This section will look at what should be done and how you should approach company research.

### *Company Background*

When looking into a company's background, it is essential to understand various aspects that shape its identity and success. Here is a breakdown to help you grasp these elements comprehensively:

- Company History: Start by researching the founding of the company, the key milestones it has reached since its inception, and any major transformations it has undergone.

- Mission and Values: Explore the company's mission statement, which typically outlines its core purpose and ambitions.
- Products or Services: Familiarize yourself with the products or services offered by the company. Understand their key features, benefits, and how they cater to the needs of their target customers.
- Target Market: Identify the target market or customer segment that the company serves.
- Key Differentiators: Research the unique selling propositions or key differentiators that set the company apart from its competitors.

### Organizational Culture

Understanding an organization's culture is crucial for aligning yourself with its values and work environment. Here is how you can expand your knowledge of organizational culture:

- Company Culture: Dive into the company's culture by researching its workplace environment, communication styles, and overall atmosphere. Be careful not to get caught up in workplace reviews like on Glass door because the ones who leave reviews are usually negative. Look for the average response to interviews that people have.
- Core Beliefs: Explore the foundational beliefs that shape the company's culture. This could include principles such as integrity, diversity and inclusion, transparency, or commitment to excellence.

- Employee Expectations: Examine how employees are expected to embody the company's values and culture.
- Communication Channels: Review the company's website, social media platforms, and any news or press releases to gain a sense of how the company communicates its values and culture to external stakeholders.
- Employee Well-Being: Explore how the company prioritizes employee well-being, work-life balance, and professional development opportunities.
- Recognition and Rewards: Look into how the company recognizes and rewards employees for their contributions.

### Recent Developments

Staying informed about a company's recent developments is crucial for demonstrating your interest and understanding of its evolving strategies and growth prospects. Here's a guide to expanding your knowledge in this area:

- New Product Launches: Keep track of any new products or services the company has recently launched.
- Partnerships and Collaborations: Research any recent partnerships or collaborations the company has announced.
- Expansions and Acquisitions: Stay updated on any expansions into new markets or regions, as well as any acquisitions the company has made.

- Financial Performance: Monitor the company's financial performance through quarterly reports, earnings calls, or analyst assessments.
- Industry Recognition and Awards: Keep an eye on any industry awards, recognitions, or accolades the company has received.
- Executive Changes and Leadership Updates: Be aware of any executive changes or leadership updates within the company.

### *Key Players*

Understanding the key players is essential for gaining insights into its leadership dynamics, decision-making processes, and overall strategic direction. Here is how you can expand your knowledge about key players within a company:

- Executive Leadership Team: Identify and research the members of the company's executive leadership team. This typically includes the CEO, CFO, CTO, CMO, and other C-suite executives.
- Board of Directors: Explore the composition of the company's board of directors. Research the backgrounds, experiences, and industry affiliations of board members.
- Key Department Heads: Identify key department heads or senior leaders within crucial functional areas such as operations, marketing, finance, HR, and technology.
- Influential Team Members: Look for influential team members or employees who are recognized for their

contributions, expertise, or leadership within the organization.

- External Influencers and Industry Experts: Consider external influencers or industry experts who have partnerships, collaborations, or advisory roles with the company.
- Track Record and Achievements: Research the track record, achievements, and notable projects of key players within the organization.
- Communication Style and Presence: Pay attention to the communication style, public presence, and engagement of key players within the organization.

### Competitive Landscape

Researching the competitive landscape is crucial for understanding a company's position within its industry, identifying opportunities for growth, and formulating effective strategies for staying competitive. Here is a guide to expanding your knowledge about a company's competitive landscape:

- Identify Key Competitors: Start by identifying the company's main competitors in the market. Research other companies offering similar products or services.
- Competitor Analysis: Conduct a thorough analysis of each competitor, focusing on their strengths, weaknesses, market share, key differentiators, and strategic priorities.
- SWOT Analysis: Perform a SWOT analysis for the company and its key competitors.

- Market Positioning and Brand Perception: Analyze their brand perception, market positioning strategies, pricing strategies, distribution channels, and customer experiences.
- Customer Insights and Feedback: Gather insights from customers, reviews, surveys, and market research reports to understand how the company's products or services are perceived relative to competitors.
- Innovation and R&D: Explore the innovation strategies, research and development (R&D) efforts, and product pipeline of the company and its competitors.
- Partnerships and Alliances: Research any partnerships, alliances, or collaborations that the company has formed with other industry players.

### Company Mission Alignment

As discussed earlier, aligning your values, career goals, skills, and experiences with a company's mission and vision is crucial for both personal satisfaction and professional success. Here is a guide on expanding your understanding of how you can evaluate the alignment between your values and career goals with a company's mission:

- Understand the Company's Mission and Vision: Start by thoroughly analyzing the company's mission statement and vision to understand its core values, guiding principles, and long-term goals.
- Reflect on Your Values and Career Goals: Reflect on your own values, beliefs, career aspirations, and

personal goals. Consider what motivates you, what values are important to you in a workplace, and the impact you want to make in your career.

- Assess Skills and Experiences: Evaluate your skills, experiences, expertise, and accomplishments to determine how they align with the requirements and objectives of the company.
- Cultural Fit: Consider the company's culture, work environment, and values to assess if they align with your own working style, preferences, and professional ethos.
- Identify Areas of Contribution: Identify specific areas where you can contribute your skills, experiences, and expertise to support the company's mission and strategic objectives.
- Personal Development Opportunities: Evaluate how the company's mission and vision align with your own professional growth and development goals.
- Value Proposition: Craft a value proposition that articulates how your values, career goals, skills, and experiences align with the company's mission and vision.
- Prepare Examples and Stories: During interviews or networking opportunities, be prepared to share specific examples, achievements, and stories that demonstrate how your values, career goals, skills, and experiences align with the company's mission.

## 4. LOOK OUT FOR RED FLAGS

The next step in your preparation process is being aware of red flags that may indicate potential issues with a company or position (Zucker, 2022). Here are some red flags to look out for:

### *Negative Employee Reviews*

Negative employee reviews can provide valuable insights into the company's work culture and management practices. If you consistently encounter negative reviews on websites, it serves as a significant red flag that warrants further investigation.

- Toxic Work Environment: Negative reviews that highlight issues such as bullying, harassment, discrimination, or a lack of teamwork suggest a toxic work environment.
- Management Problems: Complaints about poor leadership, micromanagement, favoritism, lack of transparency, or ineffective communication from managers can indicate underlying management issues within the organization.
- High Employee Turnover: If negative reviews frequently mention high turnover rates or employees leaving the company soon after joining, it suggests dissatisfaction or unrest among the staff.
- Lack of Growth Opportunities: Negative reviews that highlight limited opportunities for advancement, lack of training or skill development,

or unclear career paths within the organization may signal a stagnant or unfulfilling work environment.

- Inconsistent Work-Life Balance: Reviews that discuss long working hours, unrealistic expectations, or a culture that prioritizes work over well-being may indicate a poor work-life balance.
- Unaddressed Concerns: If negative reviews repeatedly mention issues that remain unaddressed by management despite employees raising concerns, it suggests a lack of responsiveness or accountability within the organization.

### High Turnover Rates

High turnover rates within a company can also be a significant indicator of underlying issues that potential employees should be aware of. When considering a job opportunity, it is crucial to look for signs of frequent turnover and understand the potential implications.

- Employee Dissatisfaction: One of the primary reasons for high turnover rates is often employee dissatisfaction. If employees are consistently leaving the company, it may indicate that they are unhappy with their work environment, job responsibilities, compensation, opportunities for growth, or the company culture as a whole.
- Instability and Uncertainty: A high turnover rate can also create a sense of instability and uncertainty within the organization. Constantly hiring and training new employees can disrupt workflow,

decrease productivity, and strain existing staff
members who have to pick up the slack.

- Lack of Employee Engagement: When employees are
  constantly leaving, it can be a sign of a lack of
  employee engagement. Disengaged employees are
  less likely to be motivated, productive, or committed
  to their work.

- Difficulty in Attracting and Retaining Talent: High
  turnover rates can create challenges in attracting and
  retaining top talent. Potential candidates may view a
  company with a history of frequent turnover as a
  risky or undesirable place to work.

- Potential Root Causes: When evaluating high turnover
  rates, it's essential to consider the root causes behind
  the issue. Identifying these underlying issues is crucial
  for addressing the root cause of turnover and
  implementing effective retention strategies.

### *Lack of Career Progression*

Next, you must look at the potential for career progression
and development. If you encounter a lack of clarity or transparency regarding opportunities for advancement during the
interview process, it may be a red flag indicating that the
company does not prioritize employee growth. Here are
some key points to consider when assessing the significance
of career progression in a potential job role:

- Stagnation and Frustration: A lack of career
  progression opportunities can lead to feelings of
  stagnation and frustration among employees.

Without a clear path for advancement or professional development, employees may feel as though their career growth is limited and their potential is not being recognized or fulfilled.

- Skills Development: Career progression often goes hand in hand with opportunities for skills development and learning. If a company does not prioritize career growth, employees may have limited access to training, mentorship, or resources that are essential for enhancing their skills and advancing their careers.

- Talent Retention: Companies that do not offer clear paths for career progression risk losing top talent to competitors who prioritize employee growth and development.

- Employee Engagement: Opportunities for career progression can have a significant impact on employee engagement and morale. When employees see a clear path for advancement within the organization, they are more likely to be motivated, committed, and invested in their work.

- Company Culture: A company's approach to career progression can reflect its overall culture and values. Organizations that prioritize employee growth demonstrate a commitment to investing in their staff, fostering a culture of continuous improvement, and recognizing the potential of their employees.

- Impact on Recruitment: A reputation for offering limited opportunities for career progression can impact a company's ability to attract top talent.

*Unprofessional Behavior*

It is also important to pay close attention to how you are treated during the interview process. Here's what you should look for when assessing unprofessional behavior during the interview process:

- Respect and Mutual Consideration: The interview process serves as an initial interaction between you and the company, and it should be characterized by mutual respect and consideration.
- Communication and Collaboration: Professional conduct during the interview process involves clear and respectful communication. If you encounter unprofessional behavior, such as interruptions, condescending remarks, or dismissive attitudes, it may indicate a lack of emphasis on effective collaboration and communication within the company.
- Organizational Culture: The behavior of the recruiter or interviewer can offer a glimpse into the broader organizational culture. Unprofessional conduct may be a red flag signaling a toxic or unsupportive work environment.
- Employee Well-Being: Unprofessional behavior during the interview process can also raise concerns about the company's commitment to employee well-being.
- Recruitment and Retention: Unprofessional behavior can also affect the company's ability to attract and retain top talent. Job seekers are likely to be deterred by negative experiences during the interview process

and may opt to pursue opportunities at companies where they feel respected and valued.

### Unclear Job Responsibilities

When job responsibilities are unclear, it can lead to a multitude of issues for both the employer and the employee. Here are some implications:

- Role Ambiguity: Without a clear understanding of what is expected of them, employees may struggle to effectively prioritize tasks and responsibilities.
- Conflicts: When different team members have differing interpretations of their roles, conflicts can arise. Unclear job responsibilities can create overlaps or gaps in duties, leading to misunderstandings and discord among team members.
- Performance Evaluation: Without clear job responsibilities, it becomes challenging for managers to assess employees' performance accurately.
- Goal Alignment: Unclear job responsibilities can hinder employees from aligning their individual goals with the company's objectives. This lack of alignment can result in a disconnect between organizational goals and individual efforts, impacting overall business performance.
- Job Satisfaction and Engagement: When employees are unsure of what is expected of them, they may experience feelings of uncertainty and dissatisfaction.
- Training and Development: Clear job responsibilities are crucial for identifying training needs and

developing employees' skills. Without a clear understanding of their roles, employees may miss out on valuable learning opportunities that are essential for their professional growth.

### No Opportunity for Questions

This is in addition to the behavior section above. When an interviewer does not provide an opportunity for candidates to ask questions or appears reluctant to address their concerns, it can be a red flag indicating potential issues within the organization. Here's what happens when faced with a lack of opportunity for questions during the interview process:

- Transparency and Communication: Open communication is essential in any professional setting. When interviewers do not allow for questions or seem evasive in their responses, it may suggest a lack of transparency within the organization.
- Information Gap: Candidates often use the question-and-answer portion of an interview to gain a better understanding of the role, company culture, growth opportunities, and expectations.
- Hidden Challenges or Red Flags: Employers who avoid questions or dismiss candidates' concerns may be concealing important information about potential challenges or red flags within the organization.
- Engagement and Interest: Offering candidates the chance to ask questions during an interview not only provides valuable insights but also showcases their

engagement and interest in the role and organization.

## 5. HONE YOUR SOFT SKILLS

Next, focusing on honing your soft skills can greatly enhance your chances of making a positive impression on potential employers (Herrity, 2023). Here are some key qualities and skills that most employers commonly look for in candidates:

- Communication Skills: Employers value candidates who can effectively convey their ideas, actively listen, and communicate clearly and professionally in various settings. Strong communication skills are crucial for building relationships, resolving conflicts, and collaborating with colleagues.
- Teamwork and Collaboration: Demonstrating your ability to work well in a team, contribute ideas, and support your colleagues is highly valued by employers. Being a team player, showing empathy, and fostering a collaborative work environment are essential for success in many organizations.
- Adaptability and Flexibility: In today's fast-paced and ever-changing work environments, employers seek candidates who can adapt to new situations, embrace change, and remain flexible in their approach to tasks and challenges.
- Problem-Solving Skills: Employers appreciate candidates who can effectively analyze problems, identify solutions, and make informed decisions. Demonstrating your critical thinking, analytical

abilities, and resourcefulness in addressing challenges can set you apart from other candidates.

- Emotional Intelligence: Showing emotional intelligence by understanding and managing your own emotions, as well as being aware of others' feelings and perspectives, is highly prized by employers. Demonstrating empathy, self-awareness, and interpersonal skills can help you navigate workplace relationships and interactions.

- Leadership Potential: Even if you are not applying for a managerial role, employers often look for candidates who exhibit leadership qualities such as initiative, decision-making abilities, and the capacity to motivate and inspire others.

- Resilience and Stress Management: Job interviews can be stressful, but employers appreciate candidates who can manage pressure, bounce back from setbacks, and maintain a positive attitude in challenging situations.

## 6. GET INTO THE MIND OF A HIRING MANAGER

Gaining insight into what hiring managers expect and look for in job applicants can be a game-changer (Beisler, 2015). Here are some key points to help you understand:

- Relevant Skills and Experience: Hiring managers are typically looking for candidates who possess the necessary skills, qualifications, and experience to excel in the role.

- Enthusiasm and Motivation: Hiring managers value candidates who are genuinely enthusiastic about the role and the company. Show your passion for the work, express your motivation to contribute to the team's success, and demonstrate your eagerness to learn and grow in the position.

- Professionalism and Communication: Hiring managers pay close attention to your professionalism, communication skills, and overall demeanor during the interview.
- Fit for the Team: In addition to assessing your individual qualifications, hiring managers also consider how well you will fit into the team dynamics.

## 7. GET TO KNOW YOUR HIRING MANAGER

Getting to know your hiring manager can also give you a valuable edge. To start, look for their name and job title in the job posting or on the company's website (*10 Ways to Find the Name of a Hiring Manager*, 2025). This can help you personalize your approach and tailor your answers during the interview.

If you want to take it a step further, consider reaching out to the hiring manager before the interview. You can try connecting with them on professional networking platforms like LinkedIn or reaching out via email. In your message, briefly introduce yourself, express your interest in the position, and ask any relevant questions about the role or the company.

Remember, the goal of reaching out to the hiring manager is to show your enthusiasm for the opportunity and to demonstrate that you are proactive and engaged. Keep your communication professional and concise, and always respect their time. By taking the time to get to know your hiring manager, you can better understand their expectations and preferences, which can help you prepare more effectively for the interview. Good luck!

Now that we've seen how to immerse yourself, I will discuss how to confidently showcase your skills and experiences during interviews in the next chapter. As you navigate the process, remember that selling yourself effectively requires a blend of authenticity and strategic self-promotion. By mastering the art of presenting yourself as a valuable asset to potential employers, you can boost your confidence and stand out from the competition.

# 2

## Ⓜ—MARKET YOURSELF

> *Your personal brand is what people say about you when you are not in the room.*

— CHRIS DUCKER

Welcome to the world of self-discovery and personal branding. In this chapter, I am going to dive deep into the art of marketing yourself effectively because, let's face it—you are a powerhouse of potential, and it is time the world knows it!

Before we even start talking about marketing strategies and résumé hacks, let's address the elephant in the room: self-confidence. I get it. Interviews can be nerve-wracking, résumés can feel like a chore, and the pressure to impress potential employers can feel overwhelming. But here is the secret sauce: In order for others to believe in you, you must first believe in yourself.

Repeat after me, "I am talented, I am capable, and I am worthy." Your journey to mastering the art of self-marketing begins with embracing your uniqueness, acknowledging your strengths, and owning your story. So, take a deep breath, wear your cape of confidence, and let's show the world what you are made of.

Before we get into the nitty-gritty of marketing yourself, let's address the top résumé dealbreakers that could potentially sabotage your job application (*In This Tight Labor Market*, 2018). Here are the key factors to avoid, as identified by hiring managers:

- Typos or Bad Grammar: 77%
  - Don't let a simple typo or grammar mistake overshadow your qualifications. Proofread your résumé meticulously to ensure it is flawless.
- Unprofessional Email Address: 35%
  - Say goodbye to that old, embarrassing email address from your teenage years. Create a professional email that reflects your name or initials for a polished impression.
- Résumé Without Quantifiable Results: 34%
  - Numbers speak louder than words. Highlight your achievements and impact by quantifying your results to showcase your tangible contributions.
- Résumé With Long Paragraphs of Text: 25%
  - Keep it concise and engaging. Utilize bullet points, short sentences, and clear headings to make your résumé easy to skim through for hiring managers.

- Résumé Is Generic, Not Customized to Company: 18%
  - Tailor your résumé for each job application. Research the company and job requirements to personalize your résumé and demonstrate your genuine interest in the position.
- Résumé Is More Than Two Pages: 17%
  - Less is more when it comes to résumé length. Keep your résumé succinct and relevant, focusing on the most impactful information within a two-page limit.
- No Cover Letter With Résumé: 10%
  - Don't skip the opportunity to introduce yourself. A well-crafted cover letter complements your résumé, allowing you to personalize your application and highlight your motivation.

The goal of this chapter is simple yet profound: to empower you to master the art of self-promotion. I want you to walk into that interview room with your head held high, your heart brimming with confidence, and your résumé shining like a beacon of your potential. I want you to believe in yourself, own your strengths, and convey your value to potential employers with clarity and conviction.

## 8. RECOGNIZE YOUR INNER CRITIC

In the pursuit of mastering the interview process, it is crucial to recognize the voice of your inner critic (Cherry, 2024). This internal naysayer often manifests as self-doubt, negative self-talk, and unwarranted criticism that undermines your self-worth.

*Signs of Low Self-Esteem/Harsh Inner Critic*

- Negative Self-Talk: Do you find yourself dwelling on perceived shortcomings or failures, often berating yourself for past mistakes?
- Perfectionism: Are you constantly striving for unattainable perfection, leading to feelings of inadequacy when faced with anything less?
- Fear of Failure: Does the mere thought of falling short paralyze you, causing self-imposed pressure to excel in every aspect?
- Comparing Yourself to Others: Do you habitually measure your worth against the achievements of others, oftentimes feeling inferior in the process?

*How to Defeat Your Inner Critic*

- Challenge Negative Thoughts: Confront your inner critic with evidence that disproves its disparaging remarks. Replace self-critical thoughts with affirmations that celebrate your strengths and past accomplishments.
- Practice Self-Compassion: Treat yourself with the same kindness and understanding you would offer a friend facing similar challenges. Embrace self-compassion as a shield against harsh self-judgment.
- Cultivate Positive Affirmations: Create a powerful arsenal of positive affirmations that counteract self-doubt. Repeat these affirmations daily to reinforce a mindset of self-belief and empowerment.
- Seek Support and Feedback: Engage with a mentor, friend, or supportive network to gain external

perspectives on your qualities and abilities. Constructive feedback can serve as a crucial antidote to your inner critic's toxic whispers.

- Learn from Setbacks: Recognize that setbacks and failures are stepping stones to growth. Embrace them as learning opportunities that shape your resilience and fortify your inner foundation.

## 9. REFRAME NEGATIVE SELF-TALK

Amidst the whirlwind of interview preparation, it is vital to recognize and reframe your internal dialogue (*Self-Talk*, 2019). Let's explore how to understand, combat, and ultimately transform negative self-talk into a source of empowerment as you embark on your interview journey.

### *What Is Negative Self-Talk?*

Negative self-talk encompasses the internal narrative of self-doubt, criticism, and pessimism that permeates your thoughts. It manifests as a persistent stream of disparaging comments and unrealistic expectations directed towards yourself, impacting your confidence and overall well-being.

### *Consequences of Negative Self-Talk*

- Undermined Confidence: Constant exposure to negative self-talk erodes your self-belief, leading to a diminished sense of confidence and self-worth.
- Impaired Decision-Making: Embracing negative self-talk can breed indecision and reluctance to seize

opportunities, resulting in missed opportunities for personal and professional growth.

- Emotional Distress: Harboring negative thoughts can fuel anxiety, stress, and even depression, creating mental and emotional roadblocks in your pursuit of success.

### Examples of Negative Self-Talk

- "I am not qualified enough for this job. I will never get hired."
- "I always mess things up. I am sure I will fail the interview."
- "I will never be as good as other candidates. Why bother trying?"
- "I am too nervous to speak confidently. I will embarrass myself during the interview."

### How to Turn It Into Positive Self-Talk

- Awareness and Identification: Recognize negative self-talk as it arises. Identify the triggers and patterns that fuel these destructive thoughts to gain conscious control over them (Mayo Clinic Staff, 2023).
- Challenge Negative Statements: Question the validity of your negative self-talk. Challenge these statements by seeking evidence that contradicts these beliefs.
- Replace with Affirmative Language: Transform critical phrases into affirmative, empowering statements. Focus on your strengths and past successes to counteract the negativity.

- Cultivate Realistic Expectations: Embrace a balanced perspective by setting achievable standards for yourself. Acknowledge your imperfections while celebrating your unique qualities and abilities.
- Practice Gratitude and Self-Compassion: Cultivate a mindset of gratitude and self-compassion. Acknowledge your efforts and progress, offering yourself kindness and understanding in moments of self-doubt.

## 10. GIVE AFFIRMATIONS A TRY

Affirmations can offer powerful support to help you feel more confident and prepared (Goldman, 2022). Affirmations work by reinforcing positive beliefs and thoughts, helping to reprogram the mind to focus on your strengths and capabilities. They can also help shift your mindset from self-doubt to self-assurance.

To start an affirmation practice, find a quiet space and time each day to repeat positive statements to yourself. Choose affirmations that resonate with you and address your specific areas of concern related to interviews. You can say them aloud or silently, whichever feels most comfortable for you.

Here are some affirmations for self-confidence to help you get started:

- "I am fully prepared and capable of handling any interview questions that come my way."
- "I am confident in my skills and experience, and I convey this confidently during interviews."

- "I radiate a calm and positive energy that leaves a lasting impression on interviewers."
- "I am worthy and deserving of the opportunities that come my way, and I approach interviews with assurance."

## 11. CULTIVATE POSITIVITY

Cultivating positivity can also make a difference in how you approach the process and boost your confidence. To develop a more positive attitude, start by practicing gratitude daily (Editorial Team, 2023). Focus on the things you are thankful for, no matter how small they may seem. This can help shift your perspective to one of abundance and optimism.

## 12. VISUALIZE SUCCESS

Visualization is a powerful tool to help you imagine yourself succeeding in interviews. It works by creating a mental picture of yourself performing well and feeling confident. This process helps program your mind for success, making it easier to manifest positive outcomes.

Here are some visualization techniques to help you achieve your goals in interviews:

- Create a Mental Movie: Close your eyes and visualize the interview scenario going smoothly. Picture yourself answering questions confidently, showcasing your skills, and connecting with the interviewer on a personal level.

- Use All Your Senses: Engage all your senses while visualizing. Imagine the sights, sounds, smells, and even the emotions you would experience during a successful interview. This multi-sensory approach makes the visualization more impactful.
- Practice Regularly: Set aside time each day to visualize yourself excelling in interviews. Consistent practice will reinforce positive beliefs and boost your confidence over time.

## 13. LEAN ON OTHERS

Building a strong support system is crucial because it provides you with encouragement, guidance, and a sense of belonging during challenging times like interview preparation (University at Buffalo, 2024). Your support system can consist of friends, family, mentors, career counselors, or even online communities dedicated to job seekers. Here are some tips on how to build a strong support system:

- Identify Your Needs: Reflect on what type of support you require during your interview preparation journey. Whether it is emotional encouragement, practical advice, or mock interview practice, knowing your needs will help you seek the right kind of support.
- Reach Out to Trusted Individuals: Do not hesitate to lean on friends, family members, or mentors who you trust and who want to see you succeed. Share your anxieties and goals with them, and allow them to provide the support and encouragement you need.

- Join Professional Networks: Consider joining professional organizations or online communities related to your industry or job search. Connecting with like-minded individuals can offer valuable insights, resources, and networking opportunities to enhance your interview skills.
- Seek Guidance From Career Experts: Consulting with career coaches, recruiters, or mentors in your field can provide you with expert advice and strategies to excel in interviews. These professionals can offer personalized guidance tailored to your specific needs and goals.

## 14. KNOW YOUR STRENGTHS

Understanding your strengths is essential for presenting yourself confidently and authentically (*7 Ways How to Identify Your Personal Strengths*, 2021). To identify your strengths in the workplace, ask yourself the following questions:

- What tasks or projects have you excelled in? Reflect on past experiences and consider the specific responsibilities or accomplishments that brought out the best in you.
- What feedback have you received? Think about the positive feedback you've received from supervisors, colleagues, or clients. Pay attention to recurring themes or commendations about your skills and qualities.
- What activities energize you? Identify the tasks or projects that you find genuinely enjoyable and feel

naturally skilled at. Understanding what motivates and energizes you can help pinpoint your strengths.

- What do you contribute to a team? Consider the unique skills, knowledge, or perspectives you bring to a team environment. Recognize how your contributions have positively impacted the collaborative efforts of a group.

Once you answer these questions, you will likely have a clearer understanding of your strengths in the workplace. Whether it is your problem-solving abilities, leadership skills, attention to detail, or creative thinking, acknowledging and embracing your strengths can help you effectively communicate your value during interviews. The more you recognize and articulate your strengths, the more confident and prepared you will feel when discussing them with potential employers. Remember, knowing and owning your strengths is a powerful asset in mastering the interview process. Good luck!

## 15. SET REALISTIC GOALS

When it comes to preparing for interviews, setting realistic goals can help alleviate anxiety and provide you with a clear roadmap to success (Clear, 2013). Here are some goal-setting techniques to guide you:

- Use SMART Goals: Use the SMART criteria to set specific, measurable, achievable, relevant, and time-bound goals. For example, rather than setting a vague goal like "do well in interviews," aim for a specific target such as "secure at least three interviews within the next month."

- Break It Down: Divide your overarching goal of mastering the interview process into smaller, manageable tasks. This could include tasks like updating your résumé, researching companies, practicing common interview questions, and seeking feedback from mentors.
- Prioritize: Identify which goals are most crucial for your interview preparation and focus on those first. Prioritizing your goals can help you allocate your time and energy effectively and prevent feeling overwhelmed.
- Monitor and Adjust: Regularly review your goals and progress to see if you are on track. Be flexible and willing to adjust your goals if needed based on new information or changing circumstances.
- Celebrate Milestones: Acknowledge and celebrate your achievements along the way, no matter how small they may seem. Recognizing your progress can boost your motivation and keep you invested in your interview preparation journey.

## 16. FOCUS ON YOUR "WHY"

Focusing on your "why" or purpose can provide you with a sense of direction and motivation (Warley, n.d.). Here are some ways to find your purpose:

- Reflect on Your Passions: Think about the activities or topics that genuinely interest and excite you. Consider how you can incorporate these passions into your career or professional goals to align your work with your personal values.

- Identify Your Strengths: Acknowledge your unique skills, talents, and qualities. Reflect on how you can leverage these strengths to make a meaningful impact in your desired field or industry.
- Consider Your Values: Define what is important to you in both your personal and professional life. Understanding your core values can help you identify opportunities that align with your beliefs and principles.
- Explore Experiences: Look back on significant experiences in your life, whether positive or challenging, and consider what lessons or insights you have gained from them. These experiences can often reveal important aspects of your purpose.
- Seek Feedback: Ask trusted friends, mentors, or colleagues for their perspectives on your strengths, passions, and values. They may offer valuable insights that can help you gain clarity on your purpose.

By focusing on your "why" and taking the time to explore your purpose, you can approach interviews with a deeper sense of self-awareness and confidence. Understanding the reasons behind your career goals can not only help you articulate your motivations effectively during interviews but also guide you toward a fulfilling and meaningful professional journey.

## 17. DEVELOP A GROWTH MINDSET

When facing interview anxiety, embracing a growth mindset can empower you to confront challenges with resilience and optimism (Dweck, 2015). Discover the key insights about cultivating a growth mindset and learn valuable strategies to apply it effectively.

### *What Is a Growth Mindset?*

A growth mindset involves the belief that one's abilities and intelligence can be enhanced through commitment and effort. Individuals with a growth mindset welcome challenges, persevere in adversity, view exertion as a route to expertise, and glean insights from feedback.

### *Growth vs. Fixed Mindset*

- Fixed Mindset: Embracing the belief that one's abilities are inherent and immutable. This perspective often results in avoiding challenges, surrendering quickly, perceiving effort as futile, disregarding feedback, and feeling intimidated by others' achievements.
- Growth Mindset: Adopting the belief that skills can be nurtured and enhanced through diligence, education, and resilience. Individuals with a growth mindset welcome challenges, endure in adversity, actively seek opportunities to learn and improve, and view setbacks as stepping stones for growth.

*How to Develop a Growth Mindset*

- Embrace Challenges: Instead of avoiding challenges, embrace them as opportunities for learning and growth. Embrace new experiences that push you beyond your comfort zone.
- Persist in the Face of Setbacks: Regard setbacks as mere obstacles on the path to success, not as roadblocks. Learn from your failures and leverage them as stepping stones for improvement.
- See Effort as the Path to Mastery: Recognize that hard work, dedication, and practice are crucial for progress and advancement. Appreciate the process of learning and honing your skills.
- Learn From Criticism: Instead of internalizing criticism, consider it as constructive input that can aid in your development. Utilize feedback as a tool for self-improvement and personal growth.
- Celebrate the Success of Others: Rather than feeling threatened by the accomplishments of others, regard them as sources of inspiration and knowledge. Celebrate others' success and harness it as motivation for your own journey of growth.

## 18. MAKE A RÉSUMÉ WORTH READING

One of the key steps to prepare is creating a résumé worth reading (The Muse Editor, 2014). Let's start by focusing on writing a compelling cover letter.

## *How to Write a Cover Letter*

To begin, a cover letter is your opportunity to introduce yourself and showcase your interest in the job. Here is how you can create an effective cover letter:

- Research and Personalize: Customize your cover letter for each job application by researching the company and tailoring your content to align with their values and requirements.
- Introduction: Start with a strong opening paragraph that grabs the employer's attention. Mention the specific position you are applying for and how you found out about the job.
- Highlight Your Skills and Achievements: Use the body of the cover letter to highlight your relevant skills and accomplishments. Focus on how your experiences make you a strong candidate for the role.
- Show Your Enthusiasm: Express your enthusiasm for the opportunity and explain why you are passionate about working for the company. This will demonstrate your genuine interest in the position.
- Closing: End your cover letter with a strong closing statement, reiterating your interest in the position and expressing your desire for an interview to discuss how you can contribute to the company's success.

## 19. BUILD ON TEMPLATES

If you are unsure where to start, there are various cover letter templates available that you can use as a foundation and customize to fit your personal style and the job requirements. Here are a few key points to keep in mind:

- Professional Format: Ensure your cover letter is formatted professionally with a clear structure and easy-to-read font.
- Customize: Tailor each cover letter to the specific job and company you are applying to. Mention key details that show you've done your research.
- Concise and Engaging: Keep your cover letter concise and engaging. Aim to convey your value in a clear and compelling way.
- Proofread: Before submitting your cover letter, be sure to proofread it carefully to catch any typos or errors that could detract from your professionalism.

## 20. PROVIDE YOUR PROFESSIONAL SUMMARY

It's essential not to overlook the importance of a professional summary on your résumé. Here's a guide to help you understand when to write one, how to create it effectively, and some examples to inspire you.

### When to Write a Professional Summary

A professional summary is a brief statement at the top of your résumé that highlights your key skills, experiences, and accomplishments. You should consider including a professional summary if:

- **You Want to Grab the Recruiter's Attention:** A compelling professional summary can grab the attention of hiring managers and entice them to read further.
- **You're Changing Careers:** If you are transitioning to a new industry or role, a professional summary can succinctly explain your transferable skills and why you're a good fit for the position.
- **You Want to Showcase Your Unique Selling Points:** Use the professional summary to highlight what sets you apart from other candidates and why you are the best fit for the job.

### How to Write a Professional Summary

To create an impactful professional summary, follow these tips:

- **Keep It Concise:** Aim for a summary that is around 3-4 sentences long. It should be a quick snapshot of your qualifications and what you can offer.
- **Focus on Relevance:** Highlight your most relevant skills, experiences, and achievements that align with the job you are applying for.
- **Use Action Words:** Start each sentence with powerful action verbs to convey your accomplishments effectively.
- **Show Enthusiasm:** Let your passion for your work

shine through in your professional summary, showcasing your motivation and dedication.

## *Examples*

Here are a few examples to give you an idea of how to structure your professional summary:

- Experienced Marketing Professional: Results-driven marketing specialist with over five years of experience in developing and implementing strategic marketing campaigns. Skilled in digital marketing and campaign analysis, consistently exceeding targets and driving brand visibility.
- Customer Service Manager: Dedicated customer service manager with a proven track record of enhancing customer satisfaction levels through effective team leadership and problem-solving skills. Known for implementing innovative solutions that improve customer experience and increase retention rates.
- Entry-Level IT Professional: Recent IT graduate with a strong foundation in programming languages and IT infrastructure. Eager to apply technical skills in a dynamic work environment to contribute to project success and drive organizational growth.

## 21. UNDERSTAND RÉSUMÉ ANATOMY

It's crucial to understand the anatomy of a résumé and ensure yours is tailored to make a strong impression. Here's a guide to help you grasp the key elements of a résumé, how to customize it for each job application, and why adding a portfolio and LinkedIn profile can boost your chances of success.

### Key Elements

A well-crafted résumé should include the following key elements:

- Contact Information: Your name, phone number, email address, and LinkedIn profile (if available) should be prominently displayed at the top of the page.
- Professional Summary: A brief overview of your skills, experiences, and career goals that showcases your value as a candidate.
- Work Experience: A list of your previous roles, including job titles, company names, dates of employment, and bulleted descriptions of your key responsibilities and accomplishments.
- Education: Details of your educational background, including degrees earned, institution names, graduation dates, and any relevant coursework or honors.
- Skills: A section highlighting your key skills, such as technical proficiencies, language abilities, or soft skills that are relevant to the job.

- Additional Sections: Optional sections like certifications, professional affiliations, or volunteer work that demonstrate your qualifications and interests.

## 22. TAILOR YOUR RÉSUMÉ TO THE JOB DESCRIPTION

To increase your chances of landing an interview, tailor your résumé to each job description by:

- Reviewing the Job Posting: Identify the key skills and qualifications the employer is looking for in the job listing.
- Matching Keywords: Incorporate relevant keywords from the job description into your résumé to show how your experiences align with the role.
- Highlighting Relevant Experience: Emphasize past accomplishments and experiences that are most relevant to the job you are applying for.

## 23. CREATE A BALANCED AND PROFESSIONAL LOOK

It's also important to ensure visual harmony to make a lasting impression on potential employers. Here are some tips to guide you through this process:

- Organize Your Sections: Divide your résumé into clear sections such as Contact Information, Summary, Work Experience, Education, and Skills. Each section should be distinct and easy to identify.

- Consistent Formatting: Maintain a consistent formatting style throughout your résumé. Use the same font type, size, and color for all text. Ensure that headings are bold and stand out from the rest of the content.
- White Space: Keep your résumé clutter-free by utilizing white space effectively. This helps in creating a clean and organized look, making it easier for recruiters to skim through your qualifications.
- Use Bullet Points: Present your accomplishments, skills, and experiences in bullet points rather than lengthy paragraphs. This not only makes the information easier to read but also adds to the visual appeal of your résumé.
- Visual Hierarchy: Prioritize information based on its importance. Make sure that the most relevant details, such as your work experience or key skills, stand out prominently.
- Balance Content: Distribute content evenly across the page to avoid overcrowding any particular section. Balance text and white space to create a visually appealing layout.

## 24. ADD A PORTFOLIO AND LINKEDIN PROFILE

Including a portfolio of your work samples and a LinkedIn profile in your application can provide additional insights into your qualifications and professionalism.

- Portfolio: Showcase your work examples, such as projects, designs, presentations, or writing samples, in a digital portfolio or provide links in your résumé.

- LinkedIn Profile: Create a LinkedIn profile that stands out by
  - using a professional headshot.
  - writing a compelling headline and summary that highlights your key skills and experiences.
  - including detailed descriptions of your work experiences and projects.
  - requesting recommendations from colleagues or supervisors to add credibility.

## 25. UPDATE IT DURING CAREER CHANGES

When going through career changes, updating your résumé is essential to effectively showcase your skills and experience in a new light. Here are some tips to help you navigate this process with confidence:

- Highlight Transferable Skills: Emphasize the transferable skills you have gained from your previous roles that are relevant to the new career path you are pursuing. Focus on abilities such as leadership, communication, problem-solving, and adaptability that are universally valued.
- Customize Your Résumé: Tailor your résumé to fit the requirements of the new role you are targeting. Adjust your summary, work experience, and skills sections to align with the job description and highlight how your background makes you a strong candidate.
- Reorder Your Sections: Consider rearranging the sections on your résumé to bring focus to the most relevant information. For example, if your work

experience in the new field is limited but you have relevant certifications or projects, highlight those sections prominently.

- Update Your Professional Summary: Craft a compelling professional summary that not only reflects your career aspirations but also showcases how your past experiences have prepared you for this new direction. Use this section to make a compelling case for why you are a strong candidate.

- Showcase Your Learning: If you have pursued additional education, certifications, or training relevant to your new career path, make sure to highlight these achievements on your résumé. Demonstrating a commitment to learning and growth can be highly appealing to potential employers.

## 26. USE THE RIGHT WORDS

Using the right words can significantly impact how your qualifications are perceived by potential employers. Here are some tips to help you choose the right words for your résumé:

### Avoid Certain Words

- Overused Buzzwords: Words like "hardworking," "team player," and "detail-oriented" are often overused and may not effectively differentiate you from other candidates.
- Vague Terms: Avoid using vague terms like "responsible for" or "worked on." These terms fail to

provide specific details about your accomplishments and contributions.

- Clichés: Steer clear of clichés like "think outside the box" or "dynamic self-starter." These phrases can come across as insincere and may not add value to your résumé.

### Use These Instead

- Action Verbs: Use strong action verbs to describe your achievements and responsibilities. Words like "achieved," "implemented," "developed," and "managed" can effectively convey your accomplishments.
- Quantifiable Results: Instead of vague descriptions, quantify your achievements whenever possible. For example, rather than saying "increased sales," specify the percentage or amount by which sales increased.
- Tailored Keywords: Tailor your résumé to the specific job description by incorporating keywords related to the industry, job role, and skills required for the position. This not only helps your résumé get past applicant tracking systems but also demonstrates your fit for the role.

### Be Specific

- Use Numbers: Provide specific examples of your accomplishments and use concrete numbers, percentages, or figures to quantify the impact you had in previous roles.

- Customize for the Industry: Use industry-specific terminology to demonstrate your understanding of the field and showcase your expertise.

## 27. POLISH AND PROOFREAD

Having a polished résumé is crucial to making a strong first impression on potential employers. Here are some tips to help you polish your résumé and ensure it is free of errors:

- Update Your Information: Make sure all your contact information, including your phone number and email address, is up-to-date. Ensure that your current job title, work experience, and education details are accurately reflected on your résumé.
- Format for Readability: Choose a clean and professional format for your résumé. Use clear headings, bullet points, and consistent formatting to make it easy for recruiters to scan through your qualifications quickly.
- Proofread for Errors: Before submitting your résumé, thoroughly proofread it to catch any spelling or grammar mistakes. Typos can detract from your credibility, so take the time to review your résumé carefully or ask someone else to review it for you.
- Check for Consistency: Ensure that the formatting, font styles, and bullet points are consistent throughout your résumé. Inconsistencies in formatting can make your résumé appear unprofessional.
- Tailor for Each Job: Customize your résumé for each job application by highlighting relevant skills and

experiences that align with the job requirements. This can help you stand out as a strong candidate for the specific role you are applying for.

- Use Strong Language: Use powerful and descriptive language to convey your achievements and responsibilities. Begin bullet points with action verbs to showcase your accomplishments in a clear and impactful manner.

- Quantify Your Achievements: Whenever possible, quantify your achievements with specific numbers or results. This adds credibility to your accomplishments and gives employers a concrete understanding of your contributions.

In the upcoming chapter, I will provide practical strategies to help you ease interview anxiety and approach the process with confidence and poise. Whether you are feeling nervous about upcoming job interviews or seeking to enhance your preparation techniques, I will provide you with valuable insights and tips to master the art of interview preparation.

# 3

# ℗—PREP LIKE A PRO

> *Luck is what happens when preparation meets opportunity.*
>
> — SENECA

Can you feel the adrenaline rushing through your veins as you gear up for that upcoming interview? The excitement, the nervous energy, the mix of anticipation and anxiety—it is all part of the beautifully chaotic dance that is the job search process.

It's essential to approach interviews as a two-way street, a dialogue in which both parties assess the potential for collaboration. Are you an expert at getting the interview yet keep finding new and creative ways to self-sabotage during it? Remember, it is not an interrogation; it is a conversation, a chance for you to showcase your skills and values while also gauging whether the company aligns with your career aspirations.

In this chapter, I will explore the essence of meticulous planning, strategic practice, and effective positioning to help you not just survive but thrive in the competitive landscape of job interviews. So, grab your favorite beverage, settle into a cozy spot, and let's dive into the world of preparation together.

## 28. CHECK YOUR SOCIALS

If you are looking to prep right before an interview, it is essential to check your social media presence (Guest, 2016). A quick social media cleanup can leave a positive impression on your potential employer.

Here is how you can do it:

- Review Your Profiles: Review your profiles on all social media platforms. Check your photos, posts, comments, and any publicly available information.
- Update Privacy Settings: Adjust your privacy settings to control who can see your posts, photos, and personal information.
- Remove Inappropriate Content: Delete any posts, comments, or photos that a potential employer might consider unprofessional or inappropriate.
- Highlight Professional Achievements: Showcase your accomplishments and experiences that align with the job you are interviewing for.
- Check Tags and Mentions: Review posts where you have been tagged or mentioned. Remove anything that might not reflect well on you professionally.

## 29. MASTER YOUR ELEVATOR PITCH

Next, it is crucial to master your elevator pitch (*Developing Your Elevator Pitch*, n.d.). Here is what you need to know:

### *When Do You Use an Elevator Pitch?*

You use an elevator pitch when you need to succinctly and effectively communicate who you are, what you do, and what you can offer within a short time, such as during an interview, networking event, or career fair.

### *Components of an Elevator Pitch*

An effective elevator pitch includes:

- your introduction
- your skills and expertise
- your achievements or unique value proposition
- a closing statement or call to action

### *How to Craft a Great Elevator Pitch*

- Focus on Clarity: Clearly articulate who you are and what you do.
- Be Concise: Keep it brief, ideally under 60 seconds.
- Show Your Value: Highlight what sets you apart and your key accomplishments.
- Practice, Practice, Practice: Rehearse your pitch until it feels natural and not rehearsed.

Here is a simple template for an elevator pitch:

*Hi, I'm [Your Name]. I have [number] years of experience in [industry or role], specializing in [your expertise]. I am passionate about [key interest or skill], which has led me to [significant achievement or contribution]. I am excited about the opportunity to [specific goal or contribution] at [company you are interviewing with].*

## 30. PREPARE YOUR RESPONSES FOR COMMONLY ASKED QUESTIONS

It is also essential to anticipate and prepare your responses for commonly asked questions (Indeed Editorial Team, 2023). Here is how you can effectively do this:

- Research Common Interview Questions: Take some time to research common interview questions related to your field or industry. This will give you an idea of what to expect.
- Understand the Job Description: Tailor your responses to show how your skills and experiences align with the requirements of the job you are interviewing for.
- Prepare Your Answers: Practice answering questions such as:
  - "What are your strengths and weaknesses?"
  - "Why do you want to work for this company?"
  - "Can you provide an example of a challenging situation you have faced and how you resolved it?"

- Use the STAR Method: When answering behavioral questions, structure your responses using the situation, task, action, result (STAR) method to provide a clear and concise answer.
- Practice, Practice, Practice: Rehearse your responses out loud or with a friend or family member to build confidence and ensure your answers are clear and concise.
- Make sure you have a few questions ready to ask the interviewer when they ask, "Do you have any questions for us?" Ask questions like:
  - Can you describe the company culture and how this role contributes to achieving the company's goals?
  - What qualities are you looking for in an ideal candidate, and how does this position align with the company's long-term vision?
  - How does the team typically collaborate on projects, and what opportunities are there for professional growth within the organization?
  - How does the organization support continuous learning and professional development for its employees, particularly in roles that involve content creation and educational material?

## 31. DO A MOCK INTERVIEW

Conducting a mock interview can be incredibly beneficial in boosting your confidence and improving your interview performance (*How to Conduct the Mock Interview*, n.d.). Here is a guide on how to conduct a mock interview:

### How to Conduct a Mock Interview

- Choose a Partner: Find a friend, family member, or mentor who can act as the interviewer for your mock interview. Ideally, this person should be able to provide constructive feedback on your responses.
- Select a Quiet Location: Find a quiet and distraction-free environment to conduct your mock interview. This will help you focus and simulate a real interview setting.
- Use a Structured Format: Prepare a list of common interview questions or use questions specific to the job you are applying for. Make sure to cover a range of behavioral, situational, and technical questions.
- Dress the Part: Dress in interview attire to create a more realistic experience and help you get into the right mindset.
- Record or Take Notes: Consider recording your mock interview session so you can review your performance later. Alternatively, have your partner take notes on your responses and delivery.
- Seek Feedback: After the mock interview, ask your partner for feedback on your answers, body language, and overall performance. Use this feedback to identify areas for improvement.

### Coursera Mock Interview

Platforms like Coursera provide a wide range of resources specifically designed to help individuals prepare for job interviews, including mock interview courses and tools. These mock interview resources are developed to simulate real interview scenarios, allowing you to practice and refine your interview skills in a controlled and supportive environment.

Engaging in mock interviews through these platforms offers several benefits. First and foremost, it gives you the opportunity to familiarize yourself with the interview process, question types, and common techniques used by interviewers. This familiarity can help alleviate anxiety and increase your confidence when facing actual interviews.

Furthermore, mock interview courses often include structured guidelines, feedback mechanisms, and performance assessments. These features provide a valuable framework for self-improvement, allowing you to identify areas for improvement and measure your progress over time. You can actively work on enhancing your interview performance by receiving constructive feedback on your responses, body language, and overall presentation.

In addition, the tools provided by platforms like Coursera can offer personalized guidance based on your specific career goals and industry requirements. This tailored approach enables you to fine-tune your responses and strategies, ensuring that you are well-prepared to address the unique challenges of your desired role or field.

## 32. MAKE SURE YOU ARE ON THE SAME PAGE WITH YOUR REFERENCES

It's also important to ensure you are on the same page with your references (*Tips for Choosing the Best Job References*, 2024). Here is what you need to know:

## How to Choose the Right References

- Select Relevant Contacts: Choose individuals who can speak to your work ethic, skills, and achievements in a professional setting. This can include former supervisors, colleagues, or mentors.
- Consider the Job Requirements: Tailor your selection of references based on the requirements of the job you are applying for. Choose references who can highlight your qualifications for the specific role.
- Seek Permission: Always ask for permission before listing someone as a reference. Inform them about the job you are applying for and provide them with details to help them prepare.
- Provide Context: Give your references information about the job description, the skills or experiences the employer is looking for, and specific projects or accomplishments they can speak to.

## Common Questions Hiring Managers Ask References

- Can you confirm the candidate's job title and dates of employment?
- How would you describe the candidate's work ethic and professionalism?
- What were the candidate's key responsibilities in their role?
- Can you provide an example of a significant accomplishment or project the candidate worked on?
- How does the candidate handle challenges or conflicts in the workplace?

## 33. PLAN YOUR ROUTE AND TIMING

Next, you must plan your route and timing to ensure a smooth and punctual arrival on the day of your interview (Walsh, 2023). Here's how you can find the shortest route using Google Maps:

- Access Google Maps: Open the Google Maps app on your smartphone or visit the Google Maps website on your computer.
- Enter Your Starting Point: Type in the address of your starting point, which is usually your home or the location you will be departing from.
- Enter the Interview Location: Next, enter the address of the interview location as your destination. Make sure to include the specific building or suite number if provided.
- Select Route Options: Google Maps will provide you with different route options, including the shortest route, the route with the least traffic, and other alternatives. Choose the option that works best for you based on distance and estimated time.
- Review Traffic Conditions: Google Maps will also show you current traffic conditions, including any congestion or delays along your chosen route. Take this into consideration when planning your departure time.
- Explore Transportation Options: If you will be using public transportation, Google Maps can also provide you with detailed transit schedules and routes to reach your destination.

- Save the Route: Once you have selected the best route, you can save it on Google Maps for easy access on the day of your interview. This will allow you to quickly refer back to the directions if needed.

## 34. MAKE SURE YOU'RE FUELED UP

It's crucial to fuel up with the right foods and drinks to help you stay focused and energized (Clinic, 2019). Here are some important tips:

### *What to Eat and Drink (and Avoid) Before an Interview*

- Healthy, Balanced Meal: Opt for a light and balanced meal that includes a mix of lean proteins, whole grains, and fruits or vegetables. This can help sustain your energy levels throughout the interview.
- Hydrate with Water: Drink plenty of water to stay hydrated and to keep your mind sharp. Aim to drink water throughout the day leading up to your interview.
- Avoid Heavy or Greasy Foods: Steer clear of foods that are heavy, greasy, or high in sugar, as they can make you feel lethargic and sluggish.
- Skip Caffeine: While you may be tempted to reach for a cup of coffee to boost your alertness, it is best to avoid caffeine before an interview as it can sometimes increase anxiety or jitters.

*The Best Time to Eat (Around 90 Minutes Before)*

- Timing Is Key: Aim to eat your meal about 60–90 minutes before your interview. This allows enough time for digestion and absorption of nutrients without feeling too full or lethargic.
- Avoid Rushing: Have your meal at a leisurely pace to avoid feeling rushed or bloated. Take the time to enjoy your food and focus on preparing for the interview.

## 35. GET MOVING

When you're feeling nervous before an interview, these quick exercises can help you release some of that tension (Collins, 2022).

- Deep Breathing: Take a few moments to focus on your breath. Inhale deeply through your nose, hold for a few seconds, and then exhale slowly through your mouth. Repeat this a few times to calm your nerves.
- Shoulder Rolls: Sit up straight or stand up, and slowly roll your shoulders backward in a circular motion. This can help relieve any tension in your shoulder and neck muscles.
- Neck Stretches: Gently tilt your head to one side and hold for a few seconds, then switch to the other side. You can also do some slow neck rolls to release any stiffness.
- Leg Shakes: If you're feeling jittery, sit down and shake out your legs one at a time. This can help

release some nervous energy and loosen up your muscles.

## 36. CREATE A NOTE WITH IMPORTANT NAMES AND DETAILS

Before the interview, it is also a great idea to create a note with important names and details that you can refer to quickly (*LinkedIn*, 2025). Here is what you should include:

- Interviewer's Name: Make sure you know the correct spelling of your interviewer's name and have it written down in your note. Addressing them by name can make a positive impression.
- Job-Related Terms: Jot down any key job-related terms or technical jargon that you may need to reference during the interview. This will help you speak confidently about your skills and experience.
- Company Information: Include key details about the company, such as its mission, values, recent achievements, and any other relevant information. This shows that you have done your research and are genuinely interested in the role.

## 37. GET A GOOD NIGHT'S REST

To ensure you get a good night's rest before your interview, here are some ways to help you sleep well (Glide Outplacement, 2016):

- Establish a Relaxing Bedtime Routine: Create a calming bedtime routine to signal to your body that it is time to wind down. This could involve activities like reading a book, taking a warm bath, or practicing meditation or deep breathing exercises.

- Limit Screen Time: Avoid looking at screens (phones, computers, TVs) at least an hour before bed. The blue light emitted from screens can disrupt your body's production of melatonin, making it harder to fall asleep.
- Create a Comfortable Sleep Environment: Make sure your bedroom is conducive to sleep by keeping it dark, quiet, and at a comfortable temperature. Use earplugs or a white noise machine if necessary.
- Avoid Heavy Meals and Caffeine: Try to have your last meal a few hours before bed, and steer clear of caffeine and heavy, spicy, or greasy foods that could disrupt your sleep.
- Practice Relaxation Techniques: If you are feeling anxious, try relaxation techniques such as progressive muscle relaxation or visualization exercises to calm your mind and body before bed.

## 38. MAKE SURE YOU HAVE EVERYTHING WITH YOU

To ensure you have everything you need on the day of your interview, here are some essentials to remember (Herrity, 2023).

- Résumé: Print multiple copies of your updated résumé on professional paper. Even if the interviewer has a copy, it is a good idea to have extras on hand in case you need them.

- Notebook and Pen: Bring a notebook and a pen to take notes during the interview or jot down any important information you want to remember.
- List of References: Have a list of professional references ready to provide if requested during the interview.
- Portfolio or Work Samples: If applicable to the position you are interviewing for, bring a portfolio showcasing your work samples, projects, or any relevant achievements.
- Photo ID: Carry a form of identification, such as a driver's license or passport, as some companies may require it for security purposes.
- Prepared Questions: Have a list of thoughtful questions prepared to ask the interviewer about the company, role, or team. It shows your interest and engagement in the opportunity.
- Directions and Contact Information: Make sure you have the address of the interview location, along with the contact information of the person you are meeting, in case you encounter any last-minute issues.

## 39. DRESS APPROPRIATELY

Here are some tips on how to dress appropriately for a job interview (*What to Wear to an Interview: 2022 Guide*, n.d.):

- Research the Company Culture: Before choosing your interview attire, research the company culture to understand their dress code. Aim to dress slightly more formal than the company's everyday attire.

- Professional Attire: Business professional attire is appropriate for most interviews. This typically means a suit in a neutral color (black, navy, or gray) for both men and women.
- Clothing Fit: Ensure your outfit fits well and makes you feel comfortable and confident. Avoid clothing that is too tight, too loose, or in need of repair.
- Grooming and Personal Hygiene: Pay attention to grooming and personal hygiene. Your hair should be neat, and your nails should be clean and trimmed. Avoid strong perfumes or colognes.
- Accessories: Keep accessories to a minimum. A simple watch, conservative jewelry, and a professional-looking briefcase or bag can complement your outfit.
- Footwear: Choose closed-toe dress shoes in a neutral color. Make sure they are clean and polished.
- Final Check: Lay out your outfit the night before to ensure that it's clean, pressed, and ready to go. This can help reduce any last-minute stress about what to wear.

## 40. TURN OFF (OR SILENCE) YOUR PHONE BEFORE THE INTERVIEW

Turning your phone off or switching it to silent mode before your interview is essential to maintaining focus and showing respect to the interviewer (*You're in the Middle of a Crucial Interview*, 2024). Here is why:

- Minimize Distractions: Keeping your phone on silent or turning it off completely helps minimize distractions during the interview. It allows you to give your full attention to the conversation and the questions being asked.

- Professionalism: Having your phone ring or buzz during an interview can be disruptive and may give the impression that you are not fully engaged or serious about the opportunity.
- Respect for the Interviewer: Silence your phone as a sign of respect for the interviewer and the interview process. It demonstrates your commitment to the conversation and the importance of the opportunity.
- Avoid Interruptions: By turning off your phone, you also prevent the possibility of unexpected calls or notifications interrupting the flow of the interview.
- Focus on Building Rapport: Without the distraction of a ringing phone, you can focus on building rapport with the interviewer and showcasing your skills and qualifications.

## 41. PREPARE A THANK-YOU NOTE TO GIVE AFTER THE INTERVIEW

Preparing a thank-you note to give after your interview is a great way to express gratitude and leave a positive impression (*The Job Interview Thank You Email Template You Need*, n.d.). Here are some key components to include in your thank-you note, along with a sample template.

### Key Components

- Timeliness: Send your thank-you note within 24 hours of your interview to show promptness and continued interest in the position.
- Personalization: Address the note to the specific person or people you interviewed with. Mention specific details from the interview to show that you were engaged and attentive.
- Gratitude: Express gratitude for the opportunity to interview for the position and for the time the interviewer(s) spent speaking with you.
- Reiteration of Interest: Reiterate your interest in the position and highlight why you believe you are a strong fit for the role based on the discussion during the interview.
- Professionalism: Use a professional tone and proofread your note for any errors before sending it.

### Sample Template

**Subject:** *Thank You for the Interview*

*Dear [Interviewer's Name],*

*I wanted to extend my sincere gratitude for the opportunity to interview for the [Position Title] at [Company Name]. It was a pleasure meeting with you and learning more about the role and the team.*

*I am particularly excited about the prospect of contributing to [Company Name] with my [mention a specific skill or experience discussed during the interview]. I believe my background in [relevant experience or accomplishments] aligns well with the goals of the team, and I am eager to potentially work together.*

*Thank you again for your time and consideration. Please feel free to reach out if you need any additional information from me. I look forward to the possibility of joining the team at [Company Name].*

*Warm regards,*

*[Your Name].*

## 42. TAKE A DEEP BREATH AND STAY CALM

Before your interview, it is important to take a moment to breathe deeply and stay calm (Cronkleton, 2019). Here are reasons why taking deep breaths can help with stress relief and how you can incorporate breathwork into your pre-interview routine.

### Benefits of Deep Breathing

- Calms the Nervous System: Deep breathing triggers the body's relaxation response, helping to calm the nerves and reduce feelings of anxiety or stress.
- Improves Focus and Clarity: Taking deep breaths can clear your mind, improve focus, and help you think more clearly during the interview.
- Regulates Emotions: Deep breathing can help regulate your emotions, allowing you to present yourself in a composed and confident manner.

- Boosts Confidence: Breathing deeply can help boost your confidence and center yourself before stepping into the interview room.

### Incorporating Breathwork Into Your Pre-Interview Routine

- Find a Quiet Space: Before your interview, find a quiet space where you can take a few minutes to yourself.
- Inhale and Exhale Slowly: Close your eyes and take a slow, deep breath in through your nose, allowing your abdomen to expand. Then, exhale slowly through your mouth, feeling the tension release from your body.
- Repeat Several Times: Repeat the deep breathing exercise several times, focusing on the sensation of your breath entering and leaving your body.
- Visualize Success: While breathing deeply, visualize yourself confidently answering interview questions and making a positive impression on the interviewer.
- Stay Present: As you breathe deeply, stay present in the moment and remind yourself that you are well-prepared and capable.

## 43. MAKE TIME FOR A QUICK MEDITATION

Before your interview, set aside a few minutes to practice a mini-meditation. Find a quiet and comfortable space where you will not be interrupted. Sit or lie down in a relaxed position, close your eyes, and take a few deep breaths to help calm your mind and body (*12 Quick Mini-Meditations to Calm Your Mind and Body*, 2017).

You can start by focusing on your breath, simply observing the sensation of air entering and leaving your body. As thoughts or distractions arise, acknowledge them without judgment and gently guide your focus back to your breath.

Next, you might visualize yourself walking into the inter-view room feeling calm, confident, and prepared. Envision the positive interactions you will have with the interviewer, and imagine yourself articulating your responses with clarity and poise.

As you continue with the mini-meditation, you can also incorporate positive affirmations or mantras to help build your confidence and optimism. Repeat phrases such as "I am capable and well-prepared" or "I am calm and focused" to reinforce a positive mindset.

## 44. STRIKE A POWER POSE

Before your interview, consider striking a power pose to boost your confidence and presence. A power pose is a posture that exudes strength, openness, and assertiveness. This often involves standing tall, with your shoulders back, and taking up space with open body language. Research suggests that adopting a power pose can influence your psychological and physiological state, leading to increased feelings of confidence and empowerment (Miles, 2023).

Power poses are based on the idea that our body language can affect our mindset and behavior. By assuming a posture that conveys power and confidence, you can actually trigger hormonal and psychological changes that help you feel more self-assured and capable.

Common power poses include standing with your feet shoulder-width apart, placing your hands on your hips, and standing tall with your arms raised in a V-shape. These postures are believed to convey a sense of authority and readiness.

Before your interview, take a moment to find a private space where you can strike a power pose for a few minutes. Stand in a way that makes you feel strong and confident. As you hold the pose, focus on projecting a sense of self-assuredness and readiness.

Research suggests that even just a few minutes in a power pose can positively impact your mindset, helping you face the interview with greater confidence and presence. It's a simple yet effective way to tap into your inner strength and project a confident demeanor as you prepare to meet with potential employers.

## 45. GIVE THESE ANXIETY HACKS A TRY

As you gear up for your interview in the final few minutes, consider trying these quick and unique anxiety hacks to help calm your nerves and boost your confidence (University of Colorado, 2014):

- Chew Gum: Chewing gum can be a surprisingly effective way to reduce anxiety and stress. The act of chewing can help distract your mind and provide a sense of focus, which can be calming in high-pressure situations like an interview.
- Cold Water on Wrist: Running cold water over your wrists or splashing your face with cold water can

trigger a physiological response that helps lower your heart rate and reduce feelings of anxiety. This simple and quick technique can provide a refreshing distraction and help you feel more composed.

- Power Stance: Similar to power poses, adopting a confident stance or posture can help boost your confidence and mindset before an interview. Stand up straight, shoulders back, and take a moment to feel grounded and empowered.
- Visualize Success: Take a moment to visualize yourself acing the interview, impressing the interviewer, and confidently answering questions. This mental exercise can help build your confidence and reduce anxiety by focusing on positive outcomes.
- Hum a Tune: Humming or quietly singing a favorite tune can help calm your nerves and shift your focus away from anxiety-provoking thoughts. It can also regulate your breathing and create a soothing rhythm.
- Hand Massage: Gently massaging your hands or fingers can provide a quick and discreet way to release tension and promote relaxation. Focus on each finger and joint, applying gentle pressure to help relieve stress.

In the journey to mastering the interview process, the next destination is learning to resonate with realness. As you navigate through the anxiety and apprehension that often accompanies interviews, embracing your authentic self and showcasing genuine enthusiasm and expertise becomes integral. The next chapter speaks about the power of authenticity and genuine connection, equipping you with the tools to present the most real and compelling version of yourself.

# 4

# ®—RESONATE WITH REALNESS

*I sometimes find that in interviews you learn more about yourself than the person learned about you.*

— WILLIAM SHATNER

In this chapter, I explore the power of genuine connections and leaving a lasting impression on potential employers. I will also discuss the importance of resonating with authenticity, enhancing your communication skills, and building authentic rapport to stand out in interviews.

## THE POWER OF FIRST IMPRESSIONS

Let's kick things off with a little dose of fascinating statistics about first impressions to get you in the groove. Did you know that it takes less than 30 seconds for someone to form an opinion about you? That's right—within half a minute, people have already started crafting their perception of who you are based on initial interactions (Okoronkwo, 2023).

When it comes to social relationships, a staggering 35% of individuals consider first impressions to be extremely crucial. And here's a mind-boggling fact: One-third of adults make up their minds about someone in under 10 seconds (*23 Most Interesting First Impression Statistics to Know*, 2024).

Now, what are the key elements that contribute to making a solid imprint during those precious initial moments? Well, it turns out that a friendly smile, good manners, and eye contact rank high on the list. More than half of the surveyed individuals believe that a genuine smile can work wonders in leaving a positive mark. So, next time you walk into an interview room, remember to flash those pearly whites!

Interestingly, 35% of people find it challenging to alter perceptions once they form, and over half of them trust their first impressions to be usually spot on. Moreover, a whopping 68% are confident in their ability to judge someone's character accurately (*23 Most Interesting First Impression Statistics to Know*, 2024). It's clear that first impressions are not to be underestimated!

In fact, a revealing 69% of Americans admit to forming an opinion about someone even before a single word is exchanged (*23 Most Interesting First Impression Statistics to Know*, 2024). This highlights the significance of nonverbal cues in shaping perceptions. So, don't underestimate the impact of your body language and appearance; they speak volumes before you even say a word.

My aim with this chapter is to equip you with the tools and strategies needed to not only make a positive initial impression but also maintain it throughout the interview process. By honing your communication skills, mastering the art of authentic connection, and showcasing your real self, you can create lasting impressions that resonate with potential employers long after you've left the room.

## THE FIRST IMPRESSION

## 46. REMEMBER TO SMILE

As you gear up for your upcoming interview, it's crucial to understand the significance of making a positive first impression. When you enter the interview room or join a virtual meeting, your initial interaction sets the tone for the rest of the conversation. A smile is a universal sign of warmth, friendliness, and approachability (Hailey, 2022).

Remembering to smile can help you create a sense of ease and rapport with your interviewer, which can go a long way toward building a connection. A genuine smile conveys confidence and positivity and shows that you are enthusiastic about the opportunity and genuinely interested in the conversation.

Furthermore, smiling can also help ease your own nerves and project a sense of calmness and composure, even in high-pressure situations. It can help you appear more engaging and personable, qualities that can leave a lasting impression on your interviewer.

## 47. PERFECT YOUR HANDSHAKE

Next, take a moment to focus on perfecting your handshake. A professional handshake is a crucial aspect of making a strong first impression during an interview. To give a professional handshake, start by ensuring your hand is dry and free of any items you may be holding. Approach the other person with confidence, making eye contact and extending your hand with a firm grip—not too limp or too forceful (*Six Steps to Give a Great Handshake*, 2017).

Aim for a brief, gentle shake with two or three pumps while maintaining good posture and a friendly expression. Practicing your handshake beforehand can help you exude professionalism and establish a positive connection with your interviewer right from the start. Remember, a well-executed handshake can speak volumes about your confidence and demeanor, setting a positive tone for the interview ahead.

## 48. MAINTAIN EYE CONTACT

Making proper eye contact is another key component of effective communication during an interview (*What Is Making Eye Contact?* n.d.). To make proper eye contact, aim to maintain a balance between looking directly at your interviewer and occasionally shifting your gaze to avoid appearing overly intense or disinterested. When your interviewer is speaking, focus on maintaining eye contact to demonstrate attentiveness and engagement. However, be mindful not to stare continuously, as this can be perceived as aggressive.

Additionally, if you experience eye contact anxiety, try to relax by taking deep breaths and reminding yourself that it's a natural part of conversation. Practice with a friend or family member to build confidence and develop a comfortable eye contact routine that feels natural to you. By mastering the art of appropriate eye contact, you can convey confidence, professionalism, and credibility during your interview.

## 49. MAINTAIN PROPER POSTURE

Maintaining proper posture during an interview is crucial for making a positive impression and displaying confidence (*How to Sit During an Interview*, n.d.). When it comes to sitting during an interview, there are several key practices to keep in mind.

First, ensure that you sit up straight with your back against the chair to demonstrate attentiveness and professionalism. Slouching or hunching can convey a lack of interest or confidence, so maintaining an upright posture is essential. It also helps in projecting a sense of poise and self-assuredness to your interviewer.

Next, make sure to relax your shoulders and keep them squared, as tense or raised shoulders can give off an impression of nervousness or discomfort. Keeping your shoulders relaxed contributes to an overall appearance of ease and confidence during the interview.

Additionally, it's essential to plant your feet flat on the ground to maintain stability and balance. Avoid crossing your legs, as this can appear too casual or closed off. Having your feet firmly grounded also helps in stabilizing your posture and exuding a sense of confidence and presence.

Leaning slightly forward in your chair can signal your interest and engagement in the conversation. It shows that you are actively listening and attentive to what the interviewer is saying. This subtle movement can also convey enthusiasm and eagerness, which are positive qualities in a potential employee.

## 50. MIND YOUR HANDS

Paying attention to your hand movements and gestures can significantly impact the impression you make on your potential employers (*The Power of Hand Gestures During Interviews*, n.d.). It's important to keep your hands visible and refrain from fidgeting, as this can be distracting and may convey nervousness or lack of focus. Using natural gestures to emphasize key points can make you appear more engaging and expressive, but it's essential to strike a balance and not overdo it.

It's common to feel uncertain about what to do with your hands. However, being mindful of your hand movements can significantly contribute to the overall impression you convey to the interviewer. When unsure, a simple and effective approach is to rest your hands lightly on your lap or gently clasp them together in front of you.

Resting your hands on your lap or gently clasping them together serves multiple purposes. Firstly, it conveys a sense of composure and attentiveness. This posture communicates to the interviewer that you are focused and engaged in the conversation, reflecting positively on your professionalism and interest in the opportunity.

Additionally, maintaining control over your hand movements allows you to regulate your body language, ensuring that it aligns with the confident and composed image you want to project during the interview. Excessive hand gestures or fidgeting can be perceived as distracting or nervous, potentially detracting from the impact of your verbal responses.

By consciously choosing a composed hand position, you can create a sense of calm and confidence, enhancing the overall delivery of your responses and demonstrating your ability to maintain poise under pressure. This subtle yet impactful adjustment can contribute to a more polished and professional demeanor throughout the interview process.

## 51. AVOID FIDGETING OR NERVOUS BEHAVIOR

It is crucial to recognize the impact that nonverbal cues can have during an interview. Fidgeting and nervous behaviors can inadvertently convey a lack of confidence or professionalism, potentially undermining your overall performance (McConnell, 2018). To counteract these tendencies and project an image of poise and self-assurance, it is beneficial to adopt strategies that promote composure and mindfulness throughout the interview process.

Integrating mindfulness and deep breathing exercises into your interview preparation routine is a highly effective approach to maintaining a sense of calm and confidence. By engaging in deliberate and slow breathing exercises before and during the interview, you can regulate your physiological responses to stress, promoting a state of relaxation and mental clarity. These practices not only serve to alleviate nervousness but also enable you to present yourself in a composed and collected manner, enhancing your overall professional image.

Moreover, implementing a brief pause before responding to interview questions can be a powerful tool for demonstrating your ability to approach challenges thoughtfully and deliberatively. This momentary break allows you to collect your thoughts, structure your responses effectively, and articulate your ideas with clarity and precision. By incorporating pauses strategically throughout the conversation, you convey a sense of confidence and attentiveness, showcasing your capacity to engage thoughtfully and meaningfully with the interviewer.

## 52. MIND YOUR TONE

Mastering effective communication skills, including tone of voice, is critical to creating a lasting impression during an interview (Nicholls, 2015). Your voice is a powerful tool for conveying confidence, credibility, and professionalism, so it's essential to pay close attention to how you communicate verbally throughout the conversation.

To cultivate an engaging and impactful tone of voice, it is important to start by practicing speaking clearly and confidently. Enunciating your words with precision not only ensures that you are easily understood but also exudes a sense of clarity and authority. By articulating your thoughts thoughtfully and confidently, you demonstrate professionalism and command attention from your interviewers.

Recording yourself as you respond to common interview questions can be a valuable exercise in honing your vocal delivery. By listening back to these recordings, you can assess your tone, volume, and pace, identifying areas for improvement and refinement. Pay attention to the inflection and modulation of your voice, aiming to convey enthusiasm, interest, and sincerity through your verbal expressions. Adjusting your tone to reflect your genuine engagement with the conversation can foster a sense of connection and rapport with your interviewers, demonstrating your enthusiasm for the role and organization.

Moreover, incorporating variations in your voice modulation can help you convey different emotions and messages effectively. For instance, emphasizing key points with slight changes in tone or volume can underscore their significance and capture the attention of your audience. By strategically adjusting your voice to reflect empathy, confidence, or excitement, you can infuse your responses with authenticity and conviction, leaving a memorable impression on your interviewers.

*COMMUNICATION 101*

## 53. PRACTICE ACTIVE LISTENING

Active listening involves more than just hearing words; it requires you to engage fully with the speaker and demonstrate understanding and empathy (Cuncic, 2024). To be an active listener during your interview, start by maintaining good eye contact with the interviewer to show that you are attentive and interested in what they are saying. Nodding occasionally or using appropriate nonverbal cues can further demonstrate your engagement in the conversation. Avoid the urge to interrupt and instead focus on allowing the interviewer to express their thoughts fully before responding.

An effective active listener also engages in reflective listening by paraphrasing what the interviewer has said or asking clarifying questions to ensure that you have understood their message accurately. This shows that you are paying attention and helps build rapport and demonstrate your interest in the conversation. Some useful phrases to incorporate into your active listening repertoire include "I understand what you're saying," "Could you please provide more details on that point?" or "That perspective clarifies things for me."

## 54. USE THE RIGHT VOCABULARY

Honing your vocabulary is also essential to effectively convey your qualifications and make a strong impression (*Most Powerful Things to Say in a Job Interview*, 2025). When selecting words and phrases, aim to use language that is clear, concise, and impactful. Utilizing action verbs such as "developed," "spearheaded," or "increased" can emphasize your accomplishments and highlight your proactive approach to tasks. Incorporating industry-specific terminology and buzzwords relevant to the job can demonstrate your knowledge and expertise in the field, signaling to the interviewer that you are well-versed in the industry.

In addition to choosing words that enhance your professional image, be mindful of the language to avoid during the interview. Steer clear of filler words like "um," "uh," or "like," as they can diminish the impact of your speech and make you appear less confident. Similarly, refrain from using overly casual language or slang that may come across as unprofessional. Instead, maintain a formal and polished tone by articulating your thoughts clearly and precisely.

### 55. AVOID FILLER WORDS

Be mindful of your speech patterns and avoid using filler words such as "um," "uh," "like," "you know," and "so." These words can detract from your message and make you appear less confident or professional (*Filler Words: Definition, Examples, and How to Avoid Them*, n.d.). One effective way to avoid using filler words is to practice the art of pausing. When a question is posed, take a moment to collect your thoughts before responding. This allows you to formulate a clear and coherent answer and prevents the need for filler words as you gather your thoughts.

Another helpful strategy is to engage in mock interviews and record your answers. By listening to the recordings, you can identify specific filler words or phrases that you tend to use and actively work on eliminating them from your speech. Remember, by being mindful of your speech and working to eradicate filler words, you can greatly enhance your articulateness and convey a more professional image during the interview.

## 56. READ THE ROOM

Pay attention to the body language, facial expressions, and overall vibe of the interviewer(s) to gauge their level of engagement and receptiveness to your responses (*Reading the Room Gives You an Edge*, n.d.). Are they nodding along or leaning in attentively, or are they displaying signs of distraction or disinterest? By actively reading the room, you can tailor your communication style and adjust your responses accordingly, ensuring that you maintain a strong connection with the interviewers.

Additionally, being attuned to the atmosphere of the interview can help you adapt your tone, pace, and content to effectively resonate with the individuals conducting the interview. This skill of reading the room can significantly enhance your ability to build rapport and leave a positive impression during the interview process.

## 57. DARE TO BE AUTHENTIC

Next, it is vital to emphasize the significance of daring to be authentic. Authenticity is a powerful trait that can differentiate you from other candidates and leave a lasting impression on the interviewers (Augustine, 2021). Rather than trying to conform to a perceived ideal or mold yourself into what you think the interviewers are looking for, focus on showcasing your true self. Embrace your unique background, experiences, skills, and perspectives; they contribute to the rich tapestry of who you are as a candidate. Being authentic allows you to speak sincerely about your passions, motivations, and aspirations, illustrating a genuine interest in the role and the organization.

When you choose to be authentic in your communication during the interview, you build trust and rapport with the interviewers. Genuine interactions foster meaningful connections and demonstrate your integrity and trans- parency. Moreover, authenticity lends credibility to your responses and makes your engagement more compelling and memorable. By sharing real-life examples, personal anec- dotes, and honest insights, you provide the interviewers with a deeper understanding of your capabilities and cultural fit within the company.

It is important to remember that being authentic does not mean being unprofessional or oversharing personal infor- mation. Instead, it involves presenting the best version of yourself—one that is grounded in honesty, self-awareness, and confidence. Authenticity allows you to communicate with clarity and conviction, showcasing your genuine enthu- siasm for the opportunity at hand. Embracing your authen- ticity sets you on a path to not only excel during the interview but also to find alignment with a company that values you for who you truly are. So, dare to be authentic, embrace your uniqueness, and let your genuine self shine through during the interview process.

## CONNECTING WITH THE INTERVIEWER

### 58. PROJECT TRUSTWORTHINESS

In the quest to project trustworthiness and establish a strong connection with the interviewer, mirroring their body language and communication style is a powerful and subtle technique to convey sincerity, empathy, and rapport (Gillett, 2015). By subtly matching the posture, gestures, and overall demeanor of the interviewer, you demonstrate an ability to relate and connect on a nonverbal level. This mirroring technique is based on the concept that people are naturally drawn to others who exhibit similar behaviors and tend to feel a sense of comfort and familiarity in their presence.

As you engage in mirroring, pay attention to the interviewer's body language without being overt or obvious in your mimicry. For instance, if the interviewer is leaning forward and maintaining open body language, adopt a similar posture to reflect attentiveness and receptiveness. Additionally, observe their gesturing style, tone of voice, and overall pace of speech, and strive to align your communication accordingly. This unspoken mirroring can foster a subconscious sense of connection and can convey that you are attuned to the interviewer's cues and are capable of building rapport.

Beyond mirroring, projecting trustworthiness also involves maintaining consistent eye contact, displaying active listening through nodding and affirming cues, and showcasing genuine enthusiasm and interest in the conversation. Transparency, honesty, and a willingness to engage with the interviewer's points further reinforce your trustworthiness. By engaging in active listening and responding thoughtfully, you signify attentiveness and respect for the interviewer's input, fostering an environment conducive to mutual understanding and trust.

It is important to note that mirroring should be subtle and respectful, aimed at establishing a natural rapport rather than manipulation. The ultimate goal is to build a genuine connection based on understanding and empathy. By employing this tactic alongside authentic and attentive communication, you can significantly enhance the impression of your trustworthiness and create a stronger and more meaningful connection with the interviewer.

## 59. BUILD RAPPORT

It's important to understand the significance of building rapport with the interviewer. Rapport is the foundation for a positive and meaningful conversation, and it can greatly influence the overall impression you leave (*10 Ways to Build a Rapport With Your Interviewer*, n.d.). To begin building rapport, focus on establishing common ground with the interviewer. This could involve discussing shared interests, career experiences, or connections to the company's mission or values. Finding these points of connection can create a sense of camaraderie and mutual understanding, setting the stage for a more comfortable and engaging exchange.

It's important to approach rapport-building authentically, as forced or insincere efforts can be counterproductive. The goal is to create a natural connection based on mutual respect and understanding. By engaging in genuine, empathetic, and enthusiastic conversation and seeking points of commonality, you can lay the groundwork for a successful interview that goes beyond just question-and-answer sessions, showcasing your ability to foster meaningful connections and build relationships within a professional setting.

In the next chapter, I will focus on mastering the art of engaging in interviews. It's important to understand the impact of your delivery on the overall impression you make. I will explore techniques and strategies to help you exude confidence, connect with your interviewers, and leave a lasting, positive impression.

# 5

# Ⓔ—ENGAGE THROUGH YOUR DELIVERY

> *I've learned that people will forget what you said, people will forget what you did, but people will never forget how you made them feel.*

— MAYA ANGELOU

Picture this: You're seated in the waiting area, flipping through your notes, and mentally rehearsing your responses. The minutes leading up to your face-to-face with the hiring manager are crucial, and while it is natural to feel apprehensive, remember that embracing your authentic self is the greatest asset you possess. There's a magnetism to genuine, unfiltered expressions and narratives.

Let your personality shine through as you recount your experiences and achievements. Pepper your responses with enthusiasm, humility, and authenticity. Remember, the goal is not to regurgitate a rehearsed script but to connect your personal experiences to the skill sets and values prized by the interviewer, aptly painting a vivid, multidimensional representation of who you are.

In this chapter, I will speak about the intricacies of self-presentation, storytelling, and the art of resonating with realness. With determination, positivity, and an open mind, you can craft an authentic narrative that leaves an indelible mark on your interviewers and sets you on the path toward professional success.

## 60. KNOW YOUR AUDIENCE

To effectively prepare for your interview, thoroughly research the company and gain a deep understanding of its culture and values (*Hcareers*, 2025). By immersing yourself in the company's background, mission, and goals, you can tailor your responses to showcase how your skills and experiences align with what the company is looking for in a candidate. As discussed in previous chapters, this personalized approach not only demonstrates your genuine interest in the organization but also positions you as a strong fit for its team.

As you gather information about the company, pay close attention to any recurring themes or values that are emphasized. Incorporate these aspects into your responses during the interview to show that you are not only aware of their culture but also prepared to contribute positively to it. Moreover, identify the specific pain points or challenges the employer is facing and address how you can add value by solving these issues. This tailored approach demonstrates your proactive mindset and problem-solving skills, which are highly valued by hiring managers.

When preparing for your interview, consider common traits and experiences that hiring managers typically look for, such as your ability to adapt to change, collaborate effectively with others, and deliver tangible results. By highlighting these key points in your responses, you can showcase your potential contributions to the company and stand out as a strong candidate.

## 61. TAILOR YOUR RESPONSES TO THE ROLE

It is also essential to tailor your responses to the role you are applying for. Start by carefully reviewing the job description and identifying the specific qualifications, skills, and experiences that the employer is seeking (Heller, 2023). Take note of keywords and phrases that are repeatedly emphasized in the job posting. This could include technical competencies, soft skills, industry-specific knowledge, or previous experience requirements.

Next, when crafting your responses, ensure that you align your experiences and achievements with the requirements of the role. For example, if the position requires strong project management skills, focus on highlighting your project management experience and any related accomplishments. Similarly, if the role calls for effective leadership abilities, be ready to discuss instances where you demonstrated strong leadership in previous roles.

It is also beneficial to weave in examples from your previous work experiences that directly demonstrate your ability to handle the responsibilities of the position you are interviewing for. By providing specific, concrete examples, you can illustrate how your background and expertise directly align with the role's requirements and present yourself as a well-prepared and qualified candidate.

Furthermore, tailor your responses to showcase how your unique skills and experiences can fulfill the needs of the role and contribute to the company's objectives. By demonstrating a clear understanding of the position's requirements and presenting targeted, relevant responses, you portray yourself as a candidate who is not only aware of what the job entails but also eager and capable of excelling in it.

## 62. CAPTIVATE WITH YOUR STORIES

Consider the power of storytelling in capturing the attention of your interviewers (*Mastering the Art of Storytelling*, 2024). Instead of simply stating your qualifications and skills, incorporating compelling stories from your professional experiences can provide a more vivid and memorable image of your capabilities. When selecting stories to share, focus on instances where you overcame challenges, demonstrated leadership, or collaborated effectively with a team. It's important to ensure that these stories are directly relevant to the skills and attributes the company is seeking in a candidate.

Craft your anecdotes to be concise yet impactful, with a clear beginning, middle, and end that highlight your problem-solving abilities, adaptability, and achievements. Engaging the interviewer through storytelling showcases your personality and communication and helps illustrate how you can contribute to the organization in a real-world context. By capturing their attention with your stories, you can leave a lasting impression and stand out as a candidate with the required qualifications and the ability to bring value to the team and the company.

### 63. USE THE STAR AS YOUR GUIDE

As discussed in Chapter 3, understanding and mastering the STAR method can be a game-changer in showcasing your skills and experiences effectively (Boogaard, 2024). The STAR method offers a structured approach to answering behavioral interview questions by breaking down your responses into four key components: situation, task, action, and result.

When using the STAR method, start by setting the stage with the situation, providing context for the interviewer to understand the scenario you were in. Next, describe the task at hand, outlining the specific challenge or goal you were facing. Then, delve into the action you took to address the situation, highlighting the steps you took, the skills you applied, and the decisions you made. Finally, share the result of your actions, detailing the outcome of your efforts and any lessons learned.

By following the STAR method, you not only provide a clear and structured response, but you also offer concrete examples that demonstrate your capabilities and competencies. This method allows you to showcase your problem-solving skills, decision-making abilities, and achievements in a systematic manner, making it easier for the interviewer to assess your qualifications.

You can apply the STAR method to a wide range of interview questions that require you to draw on past experiences, such as "Tell me about a time when you demonstrated leadership" or "Describe a situation where you had to work under pressure." By practicing and refining your responses using the STAR method, you can effectively communicate your skills and accomplishments, leaving a lasting impression on the interviewer and boosting your chances of success in the interview process. Remember to tailor your responses to each question, emphasizing relevant experiences that align with the job requirements and company culture.

## 64. ENSURE A SMOOTH FLOW

Another essential aspect to focus on is building a cohesive narrative that captivates the interviewer and effectively conveys your qualifications (*How to Write a Punchy Personal Story*, n.d.). To create a seamless flow in your responses, start by structuring your answers with a clear beginning, middle, and end. Begin by introducing the main point or theme you want to address, setting the stage for what you are about to discuss. In the middle section, provide detailed information, examples, or anecdotes that support your main point, demonstrating your skills and experiences relevant to the question. Finally, wrap up your response by summarizing your key points and connecting them back to the initial question or overall discussion.

To further enhance the coherence of your narrative, use transition words and phrases to guide the interviewer through your response. Words like "furthermore," "moreover," "in addition," and "on the other hand" can help connect ideas and create a smooth transition between different aspects of your story. Additionally, make sure to maintain a consistent tone and pace throughout your answers, avoiding sudden shifts or abrupt changes that may disrupt the flow of your narrative.

Practice speaking in a calm and composed manner, ensuring that each point you make leads naturally to the next, creating a seamless and engaging story for the interviewer. By taking the time to build a cohesive narrative, you not only demonstrate your communication skills but also make it easier for the interviewer to follow your train of thought and recognize the value you bring to the role. Remember that a well-structured and coherent story can leave a lasting impact and set you apart from other candidates during the interview process.

## 65. FOCUS ON QUALITY OVER QUANTITY

To steer clear of rambling and ensure your answers are concise and impactful, focus on delivering clear and relevant points that effectively showcase your qualifications (*How to Stop Rambling in Job Interviews*, 2016). Rather than inundating the interviewer with excessive information, hone in on preparing specific examples and anecdotes that highlight your skills and experiences. Practice articulating your thoughts in a structured and succinct manner, ensuring that each sentence contributes meaningfully to your response. Emphasize brevity by getting straight to the core of your message without unnecessary elaboration.

Remember that being concise demonstrates your strong communication and allows the interviewer to grasp the most essential information, ultimately leaving a memorable and positive impression.

## 66. DON'T OVERSHARE

It's also crucial to understand the importance of not over-sharing during this critical interaction (Back, 2023). While you want to be open and engaging, there are certain topics that are best left unsaid during the interview process. It's essential to avoid sharing personal information that is not relevant to the job, such as details about your family, health, or personal struggles. Additionally, steer clear of discussing controversial or sensitive topics like politics or religion, as these can potentially lead to misunderstandings or biases. Refrain from sharing negative experiences or criticisms of previous employers or colleagues, as this can come across as unprofessional and raise concerns about your ability to work collaboratively.

Remember that the focus should always be on highlighting your qualifications, skills, and enthusiasm for the role. By exercising discretion and maintaining a professional demeanor, you can ensure that you make a positive and lasting impression during the interview process. Striking a balance between being personable and maintaining boundaries is key to presenting yourself in the best possible light.

## 67. HIGHLIGHT YOUR ACHIEVEMENTS

When discussing your achievements, it's important to focus on providing specific examples that showcase your skills and the positive impact you've made (*Highlight Your Achievements*, 2025). Instead of simply listing accomplishments, provide context by outlining the challenges or situations you encountered, the specific actions you took to address them, and the tangible results or outcomes that were achieved as a result of your efforts.

When faced with the question, "What is your greatest achievement?" it is beneficial to use the STAR method to structure your response. As discussed previously, the STAR method involves elaborating on the situation or task you faced, the actions you took to address it, and the positive results that were achieved. By using this approach, you can provide a comprehensive and structured answer that clearly demonstrates your abilities and the impact of your achievements.

When discussing achievements during the interview, remember to tailor your examples to align with the requirements and responsibilities of the role you are interviewing for. This will help the interviewer see how your past successes make you a strong fit for the position. By effectively showcasing the depth and significance of your accomplishments through compelling storytelling, you can effectively demonstrate your value to the interviewer and leave a lasting impression.

## 68. CONNECT BY BEING RELATABLE

It's also essential to recognize the power of connecting with your interviewer by being relatable (Lipschutz, 2022). Building a strong rapport during the interview not only showcases your interpersonal skills but also helps create a positive and lasting impression. To be relatable, it is important to find common ground with the interviewer. This can involve engaging in casual conversation, displaying genuine interest in their questions and comments, and finding opportunities to share personal anecdotes or experiences that demonstrate your values, personality, and work ethic.

By being relatable, you can make the overall interview experience more engaging and enjoyable for both you and the interviewer. Additionally, being relatable helps the interviewer see beyond your qualifications and experience, allowing them to connect with you on a more personal level. This connection can positively influence their perception of you as a candidate. It's important to strike a balance between professionalism and relatability, ensuring that you come across as authentic, approachable, and personable.

Remember that the goal of being relatable is not to overshare or veer off-topic but rather to create a meaningful connection that can positively impact the interview process. By showcasing your ability to connect and form relationships, you can leave a strong and memorable impression on the interviewer.

## 69. KEEP IT REAL

You must also understand the nuances of staying authentic while navigating the boundaries of being truthful without oversharing (*Honesty in Interviews: Keeping a Balance*, 2025). When discussing your experiences, skills, and qualifications during the interview, it's acceptable to present them in a positive light by highlighting your strengths and capabilities. However, it's crucial to avoid exaggerating or misrepresenting your achievements or qualifications. Instead, focus on framing your responses in a way that showcases your genuine abilities while staying true to your accomplishments.

There are situations where it may be relatively acceptable to bend the truth, such as when emphasizing certain skills or experiences that align with the job requirements. For example, if you have limited experience in a certain area, you can highlight transferrable skills or your willingness to learn and grow in that aspect. This shows your adaptability and openness to new challenges while still maintaining honesty.

On the other hand, there are instances where complete honesty is non-negotiable, especially when it comes to ethical dilemmas or questions related to your work history. It's essential to be transparent about your past experiences, responsibilities, and any gaps in your employment history. Misrepresenting the truth in these situations can erode trust and credibility with the interviewer, potentially jeopardizing your chances of securing the role.

By being authentic, transparent, and truthful in your responses, you demonstrate integrity and build trust with the interviewer. This authenticity not only helps you present yourself in the best possible light but also sets a solid foundation for a professional relationship.

## 70. DON'T BE PHASED BY CURVEBALLS

When addressing gaps in your résumé or career changes during an interview, it's essential to approach these topics with honesty and positivity (*How to Explain Employment Gaps in an Interview*, n.d.). For a career gap, instead of trying to hide or sugarcoat it, explain how you utilized that period effectively. You can discuss any volunteer work, freelance projects, online courses, or personal development initiatives that you pursued during that time that enhanced your skills and knowledge. This shows potential employers that you are proactive and resourceful, even during periods of unemployment.

In the case of a career change, focus on the transferable skills and experiences that make you a strong candidate for the new role. Emphasize how your previous roles have equipped you with valuable skills that can be applied in the new industry. Highlight your passion for the new field and how your diverse background can bring a fresh perspective to the role.

When it comes to preparing for tricky questions during an interview, take the time to anticipate and practice responses to challenging inquiries. Think about examples from your past experiences that demonstrate your problem-solving abilities, adaptability, and resilience. Be prepared to provide specific instances where you have overcome obstacles or achieved successful outcomes.

If you encounter illegal questions during the interview—such as inquiries about your marital status or other protected characteristics—it's important to handle them carefully. Politely but firmly redirect the conversation back to your qualifications, skills, and experiences that are relevant to the job. Avoid providing personal information that is not related to your ability to perform the role effectively.

Remember, the key is not to be phased by curveballs during the interview process. Stay calm, composed, and confident in your abilities. Preparation, honesty, and a positive attitude will help you navigate any unexpected questions or topics that may arise, allowing you to present yourself in the best possible light to potential employers.

## 71. USE PIVOT TECHNIQUES

When it comes to pivoting during an interview, the key is to smoothly transition from a question or topic that may be challenging or uncomfortable to one that allows you to highlight your strengths and qualifications (Prichard, 2017). To pivot effectively, start by acknowledging the initial question or topic briefly to show that you have heard and understood it. Then, seamlessly shift the focus to a related subject that demonstrates your capabilities or experiences in a positive light.

For example, if you are asked about a weakness, you can acknowledge it briefly before pivoting to discuss how you have actively worked to overcome that weakness or how it has helped you develop new skills. By showing self-awareness and a growth mindset, you can turn a potential negative into a positive by highlighting your ability to learn and adapt. Another way to pivot could be to redirect the conversation towards a past accomplishment that showcases your relevant skills and accomplishments. This allows you to shift the focus towards your strengths and achievements, leaving a lasting impression on the interviewer.

Sample responses for pivoting can include emphasizing your relevant experience in a specific project or role, highlighting your unique strengths that align with the job requirements, or expressing your passion for the industry or company. By practicing how to pivot effectively, you can navigate tricky questions or topics during the interview with confidence and finesse, ultimately showcasing why you are the ideal candidate for the position. Remember, mastering pivot techniques is not about avoiding questions but rather strategically redirecting the conversation to present yourself in the best possible light and demonstrate your value to potential employers.

## 72. RECOGNIZE THE POWER OF THE PAUSE

Understanding the significance of utilizing pauses effectively can significantly enhance your communication skills and overall performance during the conversation (Zimmer, 2019). The power of the pause lies in its ability to convey a sense of thoughtfulness, confidence, and control. One key reason to use pauses is to give yourself a moment to collect your thoughts before responding to a question. This brief pause allows you to ensure that your answer is well-considered and coherent, rather than rushing through a response without fully articulating your points. Pausing can also create a sense of anticipation and draw attention to important information or key insights you are about to share, making your responses more impactful and memorable.

Strategic pauses can be particularly beneficial when addressing complex or challenging questions during the interview. Instead of feeling pressured to respond immediately, taking a moment to pause and compose yourself demonstrates your ability to handle difficult situations with composure and clarity. It can also signal to the interviewer that you are thoughtful and deliberate in your communication style, which can leave a positive impression.

Moreover, the timing of your pauses is crucial. For example, pausing after making a particularly impactful statement can emphasize its significance and allow the interviewer to absorb the information. Similarly, pausing before responding to a critical question can demonstrate that you are considering your words carefully and choosing your response thoughtfully. By mastering the art of the pause, you can enhance your communication skills, showcase your confidence, and ensure that your responses are engaging, precise, and well-received by your interviewers. Remember, the power of the pause is a valuable tool that can set you apart during the interview process and leave a lasting impression on your potential employer.

## 73. MAINTAIN A POSITIVE TONE

Mastering the art of maintaining a positive tone and using positive language when discussing weaknesses and challenges can also significantly influence how you are perceived by your interviewers (Jobsite.co.uk, 2013). When addressing areas of improvement or challenges you have faced, it's crucial to approach the topic with a mindset focused on growth and development. Instead of portraying weaknesses as failures, view them as opportunities for learning and improvement. When discussing a weakness, provide concrete examples of how you have actively worked to address it, showcasing your initiative and commitment to self-improvement. Highlight any progress you have made or skills you have acquired as a result of overcoming that challenge, emphasizing the positive outcomes of the experience.

Furthermore, when talking about challenges you have encountered, focus on the actions you took to navigate those obstacles and the valuable lessons you learned along the way. Use language that demonstrates resilience, adaptability, and a solution-oriented approach. Discuss how you approached the challenge with a positive mindset, sought creative solutions, and emerged stronger and more resourceful as a result. By framing your experiences in a positive light, you can showcase your ability to overcome adversity, learn from setbacks, and thrive in the face of challenges.

Additionally, maintaining a positive tone when discussing weaknesses and challenges can highlight your self-awareness, growth mindset, and ability to turn setbacks into opportunities for personal and professional development. It signals to your potential employer that you are proactive, reflective, and committed to continuous improvement. By using positive language and highlighting the constructive outcomes of your experiences, you can present yourself as a resilient and forward-thinking candidate who is well-equipped to handle the demands of the role. Remember, embracing a positive attitude and emphasizing your ability to learn and grow from challenges can set you apart in the interview process and leave a lasting impression on your interviewers.

## 74. SHOWCASE YOUR RESILIENCE

Remember that showcasing your resilience can also significantly impact how potential employers perceive your suitability for the role (*Answering Behavioural-Based Interview Questions*, 2024). When addressing questions related to resilience, it's essential to provide detailed examples that illustrate your ability to navigate adversity effectively. Consider sharing a specific scenario where you encountered a significant challenge at work, such as a project setback or a conflict with a colleague, and discuss the steps you took to overcome it. Highlight the strategies you used to remain focused, maintain a positive attitude, and find alternative solutions to the problem at hand.

You can also emphasize how you sought support from colleagues or mentors, how you managed your emotions under pressure, and how you stayed committed to achieving a successful outcome despite the obstacles you faced. By articulating the specific actions you took and the lessons you learned from these experiences, you demonstrate not only your resilience but also your capacity for growth and adaptability in challenging situations.

Additionally, when discussing your resilience, consider framing your answers in a way that aligns with the requirements of the job you are interviewing for. For example, if the role involves high-pressure deadlines or frequent changes, emphasize how your resilience has equipped you to thrive in dynamic environments and deliver results under pressure.

In the upcoming chapter, you will gain valuable insights and strategies to help you master the interview process and make a lasting impression on your potential employers. By focusing on ways to differentiate yourself and present your skills and experiences effectively in various interview formats, you can boost your confidence and stand out as a top candidate.

# 6

# ⑤—STAND OUT IN EVERY FORMAT

> *Trust yourself. You know more than you think you do.*
>
> — DR. BENJAMIN SPOCK

As you venture into the world of non-face-to-face interviews, it's perfectly normal to feel a rush of nerves and uncertainty. But don't worry; this chapter is your beacon of light guiding you through the intricacies of virtual interviews.

Imagine yourself as a digital chameleon, seamlessly adapting to each interview format and exuding confidence and professionalism with every interaction. Whether you're facing a live video interview with a hiring manager, a phone screening with a recruiter, or an asynchronous video assessment, you have the power to shine brightly and leave a memorable mark that sets you apart from the crowd. By honing your skills in communication, presentation, and technology, you can navigate the virtual interview landscape with ease and poise, demonstrating your readiness and suitability for the role.

Let's kick things off with some eye-opening statistics about online interviews that will have you nodding in agreement. Did you know that interviewers often size you up within the first 7 minutes of the interview? Yes, that's like the blink of an eye in the grand scheme of things! And get this: A 5-minute live video interview can feel as intense as attempting a 200-question test. However, video interviews have a silver lining—they're six times faster than phone calls, making the hiring process a breeze. However, as with any tech-driven endeavor, bumps in the road can occur, with 7 out of 10 candidates missing out on job opportunities due to pesky tech glitches during video interviews (D'Souza, 2024).

As you venture ahead on this journey to master the non-face-to-face interview process, it's crucial to understand the unique dynamics and nuances that these formats entail. Video interviews, phone screenings, and other virtual assessment methods require a different approach and level of preparation compared to traditional in-person interviews. The goal of this chapter is to equip you with the tools, tips, and strategies to excel in every format, ensuring that you make a lasting impression on your potential employers and stand out from the competition.

## 75. UNDERSTAND THE PROS AND CONS

When it comes to phone interviews, one major advantage is the convenience they offer (*Phone Interviews vs. In-Person Interviews*, n.d.). You can participate in the interview from the comfort of your own space, eliminating the need for travel and the associated preparation for the visual aspect. This can be especially beneficial if you're interviewing for positions in different cities or even countries. However, one potential downside of phone interviews is the absence of visual cues. Without the opportunity to convey your enthusiasm and confidence through body language and facial expressions, it can be challenging to make as strong of an impression as you would in a face-to-face interaction.

On the other hand, virtual interviews present a balance between the convenience of a phone interview and the visual engagement of an in-person meeting. Through platforms like Zoom or Skype, you have the opportunity to establish a meaningful visual connection with the interviewer. This can allow for more in-depth interaction and provide you with the chance to showcase your professionalism and personality through nonverbal communication. Despite these advantages, virtual interviews come with their own set of potential drawbacks. Technical glitches, such as internet connectivity issues or malfunctioning software, can disrupt the flow of the interview and create an unfavorable impression. Additionally, distractions in your environment, like noise or interruptions, may detract from the professionalism of the interaction.

Understanding these pros and cons empowers you to approach each interview format strategically. For phone interviews, you may choose to focus on articulating your thoughts clearly and concisely, compensating for the lack of visual cues with your vocal inflections and tone. In preparation for virtual interviews, you can address potential technical issues by testing your equipment and ensuring a distraction-free environment. By embracing the benefits and proactively mitigating the challenges of each format, you can adapt your approach and maximize your effectiveness, thereby increasing your chances of making a positive and lasting impression.

## 76. DRESS PROFESSIONALLY (EVEN IF YOU'RE NOT MEETING IN PERSON)

As you prepare for your virtual interview, it is crucial to prioritize dressing professionally, even though you will not be meeting the interviewer in person (*How to Ace Your Virtual Interview*, 2024). Your choice of attire holds significant importance as it will shape the interviewer's perception of your professionalism and readiness for the role. Striking a balance between being polished and comfortable is key when deciding what to wear for the virtual interview.

For a virtual interview, it is recommended to opt for business casual attire. This could include a crisp button-down shirt, a professional blouse, or a tailored blazer paired with neat and presentable bottoms. By choosing business casual attire, you can convey a sense of professionalism while still being comfortable in the virtual setting. It is important to avoid overly casual clothing, distracting patterns, or loud colors that may take attention away from your qualifications and presentation.

Apart from selecting the right clothing, paying attention to grooming and appearing well-put-together can further enhance your professional image during the virtual interview. Ensure that your hair is neatly styled and your overall grooming is on point to create a positive impression.

Remember that dressing appropriately demonstrates your respect for the opportunity and helps boost your confidence, enabling you to present yourself in the best possible light.

## 77. LEARN THE VIRTUAL HANDSHAKE

Learning the virtual handshake is a crucial aspect of preparing for a remote interview (McKee, 2015). In the absence of a physical handshake, your initial interaction with the interviewer via video conferencing serves as the virtual equivalent. To create a positive impression, it's essential to maintain eye contact by looking directly at the camera, as this simulates direct eye contact with the interviewer. Smiling warmly and confidently can help convey your enthusiasm and establish a friendly rapport.

Active listening, demonstrated through nodding and responding appropriately to the conversation, showcases your engagement and interest in the discussion. Additionally, paying attention to your virtual background is vital; ensure it is professional and devoid of any distractions that could draw attention away from the conversation. By mastering the virtual handshake, you can effectively set the tone for a successful interview and leave a lasting impression on the interviewer.

## 78. TEST YOUR EQUIPMENT

It's also essential to thoroughly test your equipment to ensure a seamless and successful virtual meeting (*How to Test Your Tech for a Video Interview*, 2024). Begin by checking your internet connection to guarantee that it is stable and capable of supporting a video call without interruptions. Next, assess your camera and microphone to ensure they are functioning properly. Consider conducting a test call with a friend or family member to verify that your audio and video settings are working correctly, allowing you to be clearly seen and heard during the interview.

In addition to the technical aspects, pay attention to your surroundings and lighting. Choose a well-lit and quiet space for the interview to minimize distractions and ensure that you are clearly visible to the interviewer. Position your camera at eye level to create a professional and natural look, helping you establish a confident and engaging presence during the virtual interaction.

By doing all this, you can avoid any potential technical glitches during the interview, presenting yourself in a professional and polished manner and leaving a positive impression on the interviewer. This preparation will also boost your confidence, allowing you to focus on showcasing your qualifications and skills without distractions.

## 79. MASTER THE MUTE BUTTON

Mastering the mute button and understanding mute etiquette are essential aspects of navigating the virtual interview landscape with professionalism and poise (*Silence Is Golden*, 2023). Before the interview commences, take a moment to ensure your mute button is in proper working order. Familiarize yourself with the controls and functionalities to facilitate seamless usage during the conversation.

Mute etiquette is a crucial element of maintaining a professional image. When not speaking, it's essential to utilize the mute button to minimize background noise and potential distractions. This demonstrates your attentiveness and consideration for the interviewer and fellow participants. However, remember to promptly unmute yourself when it's time to speak, ensuring that your contributions are clearly heard and understood.

Proper use of the mute button reflects your attention to detail and respect for others' time, ultimately contributing to a smoother and more focused interview experience. By mastering mute etiquette, you can showcase your professionalism and technical acumen, leaving a positive and lasting impression on the interviewer.

## 80. SET THE SCENE

Creating a professional background for your virtual interactions is a crucial step in ensuring a positive impression on the interviewer (Pelta, 2022). Begin by selecting a quiet and well-lit space with minimal distractions to serve as your backdrop. A clutter-free environment can help maintain focus and convey a sense of organization and professionalism. Consider setting up your background against a plain wall or a bookshelf, keeping the area neat and visually appealing.

Lighting plays a significant role in how you are perceived during the interview. Natural light is ideal, but if that's not available, consider using soft, indirect lighting to illuminate your face evenly and avoid harsh shadows. Position yourself in front of the light source to ensure that your face is well-lit and clearly visible to the interviewer. Additionally, it is advisable to avoid sitting with a window directly behind you, as this can create a distracting glare.

Adding a touch of personality to your background can help showcase your individuality while maintaining a professional look. Consider incorporating a plant, a piece of artwork, or professional-looking décor that reflects your interests and personality. Keep in mind that the goal is to strike a balance between professionalism and personal touch in your background setup. This visual representation of your environment can contribute to a positive first impression and help you stand out as a polished and professional candidate during the virtual interview.

## 81. MAKE SURE YOU LOOK YOUR BEST

It's also crucial to ensure that you present yourself in the best possible light during virtual interactions (theK, 2013). Lighting and framing play pivotal roles in achieving a professional and engaging appearance on camera. When it comes to lighting, aim for natural, diffused light that evenly illuminates your face. Position yourself facing a window to leverage natural light, or consider investing in a ring light or softbox to achieve a flattering and well-lit look. Avoid sitting with a light source directly behind you, as this can create distracting shadows and glare.

Additionally, focusing on the framing of your video feed can significantly impact your presentation. Position your webcam at eye level to create a natural and balanced view. Adjust the angle and distance to capture your head and shoulders, allowing the interviewer to see your expressions and gestures clearly. A well-composed frame enhances your presence and provides a professional and engaging visual experience for the interviewer.

Strategic positioning of your webcam also contributes to creating a polished appearance. Ensure that your webcam is stable and positioned directly in front of you, preventing any unsteady or distracting camera movements. Centering yourself in the frame and maintaining good posture will further convey confidence and professionalism.

## 82. MAKE SURE YOU'RE HEARD

Paying attention to several key factors can boost the audio quality of your virtual interviews, especially on platforms like Zoom (Barraza, 2023). First, it's crucial to choose a quiet and well-lit space for your interview. Background noise can be distracting and impact the clarity of your audio, so try to find a location where you won't be interrupted by loud noises.

Investing in a good pair of headphones with a built-in microphone can significantly improve your audio quality. Headphones with noise-canceling features can help reduce any external noise interference, allowing your voice to come through clearly. Make sure the microphone is positioned close to your mouth but not too close to avoid distortion.

Adjusting the microphone settings on your device is another important step. Check the input volume levels on your computer and adjust them to ensure your voice is not too soft or too loud. It's a good idea to do a test call with a friend or family member to check the sound quality and make any necessary adjustments before your actual interview.

Lastly, remember to speak clearly and enunciate your words during the interview. Speaking too quickly or mumbling can make it difficult for the interviewer to understand you clearly. Take your time to articulate your words and thoughts effectively, which will not only improve audio quality but also demonstrate your communication skills.

## 83. BE PREPARED FOR TECHNICAL DIFFICULTIES

You must also anticipate and prepare for potential technical difficulties that may occur during a virtual meeting (*What Do You Do If Your Virtual Interviewee Has Technical Difficulties?* 2024). Start by conducting a thorough check of your internet connection and ensure its stability. Test the speed and reliability of your connection to minimize the risk of dropouts or lags during the interview. Consider having a backup plan in place, such as a mobile hotspot or an alternative location with a more reliable internet signal, so you can quickly switch to a secondary connection if needed.

Familiarize yourself with the video conferencing platform that will be used for the interview, whether it's Zoom, Microsoft Teams, or another application. Take the time to learn the platform's features and functionalities, including troubleshooting options for audio and video issues. This will help you address any technical problems swiftly and efficiently should they arise during the interview.

It's important to remain calm and composed if technical difficulties occur during the interview. Inform the interviewer about the issue and be proactive in finding a solution. Offer to troubleshoot the problem together, or suggest rescheduling the interview or switching to a different communication method, such as a phone call, if necessary. Demonstrating your ability to handle unexpected challenges with professionalism and flexibility can actually be a positive reflection of your problem-solving skills and adaptability.

## 84. CREATE A CHEAT SHEET

Creating a cheat sheet can be a valuable tool to help you stay organized, focused, and confident during your conversation with the interviewer (*How to Create a Virtual Interview Cheat Sheet*, 2024). When designing your cheat sheet, it's essential to strike a balance between providing key information and keeping it concise and easy to reference. Start by including essential details such as the company's background, mission, and values to demonstrate your knowledge and interest in the organization.

Additionally, make sure to include the interviewer's name, title, and any relevant information about their role within the company. This personal touch can help you establish a connection and tailor your responses accordingly. Consider listing out specific talking points or key achievements related to your experience, skills, and qualifications that you want to highlight during the interview. These points can serve as a quick reference guide to ensure you cover all the important aspects of your background effectively.

Incorporating anecdotes, stories, or examples that showcase your accomplishments and demonstrate your problem-solving skills can also be beneficial. By providing specific examples of how you have tackled challenges or achieved success in past roles, you can make your responses more engaging and memorable for the interviewer.

Moreover, crafting a list of thoughtful questions for the interviewer can demonstrate your genuine interest in the position and the company. Consider asking about the company culture, career development opportunities, or specific projects to show that you are invested in learning more about the role and how you can contribute to the team.

## 85. BE AWARE OF TIME ZONES

Being aware of time zones is a critical aspect to consider to ensure you manage your schedule effectively (*Ensure a Successful Virtual Interview by Mastering Time Zone Scheduling*, 2024). Start by confirming the exact time of your interview and identifying the time zone in which it is scheduled to take place. Take into account any potential differences between your local time and the interviewer's time zone to prevent any confusion or misunderstandings. Utilize online tools or applications to easily convert time zones and set reminders or alarms to ensure you are ready and available at the correct time.

If you are scheduling an interview across different regions or countries, it's essential to proactively account for any time zone discrepancies and plan accordingly. Consider reaching out to the interviewer or the company's HR department to confirm the interview time in both your local time and theirs to avoid any scheduling conflicts. Additionally, make sure to factor in any potential daylight-saving time adjustments that may impact the timing of your interview.

## 86. JOIN (A FEW MINUTES) EARLY

Arriving a few minutes early, typically around 5-10 minutes before the scheduled interview time, is recommended to ensure a smooth and seamless start to the conversation (Chan, 2024). Logging in early allows you ample time to address any potential technical issues that may arise, such as audio or video connectivity issues, ensuring that you can resolve them before the interview officially begins.

Being early also demonstrates your punctuality, preparedness, and respect for the interviewer's time. It gives you the opportunity to compose yourself, review key points, and mentally prepare for the interview, putting you in a positive mindset as you approach the conversation. Additionally, joining early allows you to greet the interviewer promptly, showcasing your professionalism and eagerness for the opportunity.

Utilize the extra time before the interview to conduct a final technology check, ensuring that your microphone, camera, and internet connection are all functioning properly. Familiarize yourself with the virtual platform's features and layout, ensuring that you are comfortable navigating the interface during the interview.

## 87. CONNECT THROUGH THE SCREEN

Focusing on connecting through the screen is crucial in making a positive impression (Jezra, 2020). As already discussed, begin by ensuring you have a stable internet connection and a quiet, well-lit space where you won't be interrupted. Dressing professionally, even for a virtual interview, shows respect for the opportunity and helps you feel more confident. Pay attention to your posture, sitting up straight to convey professionalism and engagement.

Practicing speaking clearly and concisely beforehand can help you articulate your thoughts effectively during the interview. Remember to look directly at the camera to maintain eye contact with the interviewer, simulating a face-to-face interaction. This can help build rapport and convey your interest in the conversation.

Engaging with the interviewer by asking thoughtful questions demonstrates your interest in the company and the role. It also showcases your critical thinking skills and enthusiasm for the opportunity. Finally, be sure to let your passion for the job shine through your responses and demeanor, as enthusiasm can leave a lasting impact on the interviewer. By focusing on connecting through the screen, you can make a strong impression and increase your chances of success in the interview.

## 88. DO A MOCK INTERVIEW

Consider doing a mock interview to fine-tune your preparation (*Conduct a Mock Interview Online in 5 Steps*, 2024). Find a friend, family member, or mentor who can act as the interviewer and simulate the interview experience. Alternatively, you can use online resources or professional coaching services that offer mock interview sessions. Treat it like a real interview, dressing professionally and setting up a quiet, well-lit space for the session.

During the mock interview, focus on practicing your responses to common interview questions, emphasizing your strengths and addressing any potential weaknesses. Pay attention to your body language, maintaining good posture and using positive gestures to convey confidence. Work on the tone and clarity of your voice and practice using active listening skills to engage with the interviewer.

After the mock interview, seek feedback on your performance. Ask for honest insights on areas where you excelled and where you could improve. Use this feedback to make necessary adjustments to your responses, demeanor, and overall interview approach. The mock interview provides a safe space to work out any nervousness, refine your answers, and build the confidence you need to perform well in the actual interview.

In the upcoming chapter, I will introduce strategies to help ease your anxiety and master the interview process. I understand that interviews can be nerve-wracking, but with the right approach and preparation, you can confidently navigate through the final stages of securing the job opportunity.

# 7

# Ⓢ—SEAL THE DEAL

> *In business, you don't get what you deserve; you get what you negotiate.*
>
> — CHESTER L. KARRASS

Are you feeling the jitters as you approach the crucial moment when the job offer is on the table? Negotiating a salary and wrapping up an interview can be nerve-wracking for anyone. This chapter will equip you with confidence, strategies, and techniques to help you seal the deal, leaving you and your potential employer with big smiles on your faces.

Did you know that approximately 66% of U.S. employees who tried to negotiate their initial salaries reported success? It's also heartening to know that the majority of employers, around 73%, anticipate a salary negotiation from job applicants (Overvest, 2022). This means that negotiation is not just a possibility but almost an expectation. Moreover, understanding that some employers only publish salary ranges between 25 and 75% of what they actually pay for a given position indicates that there is often room to maneuver (Overvest, 2022).

The stats also show us that gender is not a barrier when it comes to negotiation—women negotiate almost as much as men, at a rate of 60% and 68%, respectively (Overvest, 2022). This reiterates the fact that anyone can be an effective negotiator if armed with the right tools and mindset.

In this chapter, my aim is crystal clear—to arm you with negotiation strategies to effectively navigate salary discussions and provide you with proven techniques to wrap up an interview on a strong note. By doing so, I intend to maximize your chances of securing the role you desire while leaving a positive, lasting impression on the hiring team.

## 89. ASK THOUGHTFUL QUESTIONS

As you stand on the brink of an important interview, poised to make a lasting impression, remember that asking thoughtful questions can deepen your understanding of the role and demonstrate your sincere interest in the opportunity at hand (The Muse Editor, 2013). The questions you pose to the hiring manager should showcase your enthusiasm for the position while also providing you with essential information to assess whether the role aligns with your career objectives. Consider inquiring about the company's future plans and how the role contributes to those goals, delve into the dynamics of the team you'll be working with, or explore the manager's leadership style to gain insights into the work environment. By asking strategic and insightful questions, you not only engage in a meaningful dialogue but also position yourself as a proactive and curious candidate who is genuinely invested in the organization.

Furthermore, knowing your professional worth is paramount as you navigate the interview process. Conduct thorough research to understand the typical salary range for similar positions in your industry and geographical location. This knowledge equips you with a solid foundation for negotiating a fair and competitive salary package. Understanding your market value empowers you to advocate for yourself confidently during the negotiation phase and ensures that you are appropriately compensated for your skills, experience, and contributions.

By arming yourself with thoughtful questions for the hiring manager and a firm grasp of your professional value, you enter the interview room well-prepared and self-assured. This combination of insightful inquiry and self-awareness not only enhances your performance during the interview but also positions you as a strong candidate who is proactive, informed, and confident in their abilities. Embrace the opportunity to showcase your curiosity, strategic thinking, and self-worth as you embark on this pivotal step in your career journey.

*KNOW YOUR WORTH*

## 90. RESEARCH THE JOB'S FAIR MARKET VALUE

It's also essential to invest some time in researching the fair market value for the position you are pursuing (Lowe-MacAuley, 2023). This step is crucial because it ensures that you have a clear understanding of your value in the job market and can confidently negotiate a fair salary. Start by examining the average salaries for similar roles within your industry or field. Websites like Glassdoor, Indeed, and PayScale can provide valuable insights into the typical compensation packages for your desired position. Take into account the regional variances in salaries as well, as the cost of living and job market conditions can impact the fair market value of a role.

Additionally, consider your own qualifications, experience, and any specialized skills you bring to the table. This self-assessment will help you gauge where you stand in comparison to industry standards. Armed with this knowledge, you'll be well-prepared to discuss compensation during the interview process and can communicate your value effectively to potential employers. Understanding your worth sets the stage for a successful negotiation and ensures that you are positioned to receive a competitive and equitable offer.

## 91. PRACTICE YOUR PITCH

Dedicating time to practicing your pitch for salary negotiation can significantly enhance your confidence and effectiveness during discussions (*The Ultimate Salary Negotiation Script for Every Scenario*, 2024). Begin by crafting a compelling introduction that highlights your key qualifications, accomplishments, and the value you bring to the prospective role and organization.

For instance, you could start by saying, "I am excited about the opportunity to contribute my extensive experience in [specific skill or industry] to drive success in this role." Transition into discussing your salary expectations by stating, "Based on my research and the scope of responsibilities outlined, I am seeking a salary in the range of [your desired salary range] to reflect my expertise and contributions." Be prepared to justify your requested compensation with tangible examples of how your skills and achievements align with the position's requirements and industry standards.

Here are a few sample salary negotiation scripts to help guide your conversations:

- Initiating the Salary Discussion: "I appreciate the opportunity to discuss compensation. Based on my research and the value I believe I can bring to the team, I am targeting a salary range of [insert range] for this role."
- Emphasizing Your Value: "I bring [specific skills or accomplishments] to this role, which I believe will significantly impact [company/project/goals]. This level of expertise warrants a compensation package that aligns with the market value for similar positions."
- Responding to Pushback: "I understand that salary negotiation is a collaborative process. While my focus is on contributing meaningfully to the team's

success, I hope we can find a compensation package that reflects both the role's requirements and my experience."

## 92. UNDERSTAND THE BASICS OF NEGOTIATION

Understanding the basics of negotiation can be a game-changer in your approach to the discussion, especially regarding salary matters (Yasmina, 2024). Understanding negotiation strategies can empower you to navigate the conversation with finesse. Begin by setting clear objectives for the negotiation, outlining your ideal outcome while remaining open to potential compromises.

Actively listening to the other party's perspective not only helps you better understand their needs but also allows you to tailor your responses effectively. Maintaining a positive and professional demeanor throughout the negotiation can contribute to constructive dialogue and foster a collaborative atmosphere for reaching a mutually beneficial agreement.

Incorporating specific strategies and tips can enhance your ability to advocate for fair compensation during salary negotiation. The negotiation process typically unfolds in several stages: preparation, opening discussions, bargaining, and finalizing an agreement. During the preparation stage, research industry standards and company policies to establish a reasonable salary range based on your qualifications and experience. When opening discussions, clearly articulate your value proposition by highlighting your skills, accomplishments, and what you bring to the role.

In the bargaining stage, consider presenting your desired salary range as an anchor point for the negotiation while remaining open to flexibility. Emphasize the unique contributions you can make to the organization as a compelling reason for deserving your target salary. Throughout the negotiation, maintain a positive and collaborative attitude, actively listen to the employer's perspective, and seek common ground to reach a satisfactory resolution.

### 93. ANTICIPATE PUSHBACK

It's also essential to prepare for the possibility of encountering pushback, especially during discussions regarding salary, experience, or certain aspects of the role (Madell, 2021). Anticipating pushback showcases your proactive mindset and your ability to address challenges with professionalism and composure. When faced with pushback during the interview, it's crucial to respond in a manner that demonstrates your ability to handle difficult situations effectively while maintaining a positive and collaborative demeanor.

One effective way to respond professionally to pushback is to acknowledge the concerns raised by the interviewer. Actively listen to their feedback and ensure that you understand their perspective. Provide thoughtful and well-structured responses that address the specific points of pushback. If the pushback concerns your qualifications or experience, be prepared to offer additional details, examples, or anecdotes that exemplify your expertise and achievements. This approach can help alleviate any reservations and reinforce your suitability for the role.

Maintain composure and confidence in your responses, even when facing challenging questions or objections. Emphasize your willingness to engage in constructive dialogue and collaborate with the interviewer to find mutually beneficial solutions. This will showcase your ability to handle adversity while maintaining a professional and positive attitude.

Moreover, consider framing your responses in a way that underscores the value you bring to the role and the organization. Highlight specific accomplishments, relevant skills, and unique perspectives that set you apart as a top candidate. By articulating your value proposition in a compelling manner, you can effectively address pushback and reaffirm your qualifications.

Ultimately, responding professionally to pushback during the interview showcases your communication skills and ability to handle challenging situations. It also positions you as a resilient and adaptable candidate. By engaging in constructive dialogue and addressing concerns professionally, you can leave a lasting impression on the interviewer and demonstrate your readiness to navigate complex scenarios in the workplace.

## 94. DEAL WITH UNSUCCESSFUL NEGOTIATIONS

When navigating unsuccessful negotiations during the interview process, it is crucial to handle the situation with professionalism and grace (Magazine, 2022). Whether you accept a job offer after a failed negotiation or turn down an offer while maintaining positive relations, how you communicate can significantly impact your professional reputation.

If you choose to accept a job offer despite unsuccessful negotiations, it is important to express your enthusiasm for the opportunity while also addressing the negotiation aspect. By acknowledging the previous discussions on compensation and expressing your hope for future reconsideration, you demonstrate your appreciation for the offer while subtly leaving room for future discussions. A diplomatic approach to accepting the offer could involve saying something like, "I am thrilled to accept the job offer and excited about the chance to contribute to the team. During our previous discussions, we explored certain aspects of the compensation package, and while I understand the constraints, I hope we can revisit this in the future as I continue to grow in the role."

On the other hand, if you opt to decline a job offer without burning bridges, it is essential to express gratitude for the opportunity and convey your decision in a respectful manner. By thanking the employer for the offer and the interview process and explaining your decision to pursue a different opportunity that aligns more closely with your long-term career goals, you show appreciation for their time and consideration. A gracious way to decline the offer could be by saying, "Thank you for the job offer and the opportunity to interview with your company. After careful consideration, I have decided to pursue a different opportunity that aligns more closely with my long-term career goals. I truly appreciate your time and consideration throughout this process."

In both situations, gracefully handling unsuccessful negotiations and declining offers can help preserve your professional reputation and open the door to potential future opportunities. By maintaining a positive tone, expressing gratitude, and allowing room for future interactions, you can navigate these challenging circumstances with professionalism and tact.

## 95. MAKE A GRACEFUL EXIT

Making a graceful exit is a key component of leaving a lasting impression on the interviewers (*10 Closing Statements to Use after an Interview*, n.d.). Your closing statement serves as the final opportunity to reinforce your suitability for the position and your enthusiasm for the opportunity. It is important to express genuine gratitude for being considered for the role and for the time and effort invested by the interview panel. Reiterate your interest in the position by summarizing how your skills and experiences align with the requirements of the role. Emphasize your eagerness to contribute to the company and showcase your excitement about the possibility of joining the team.

Additionally, expressing your willingness to learn and grow within the organization can demonstrate your commitment and dedication. By concluding the interview with confidence, professionalism, and a positive attitude, you can leave a lasting impression that sets you apart from other candidates. Remember that a well-crafted closing statement can leave a strong final impression and potentially influence the interviewer's decision in your favor.

## 96. FOLLOW UP

You should also remember the importance of doing a follow-up to reiterate your interest in the position and express gratitude for the opportunity (Somanathan, 2024). Sending a follow-up email is a professional way to show appreciation for the interview and keep yourself on the interviewer's radar. In the email, thank the interviewer for their time and reiterate your interest in the role. You can also include specific points discussed during the interview that showcase your qualifications and enthusiasm for the position. Additionally, a follow-up call can further demonstrate your interest and proactive approach.

When making the call, politely inquire about the timeline for a decision and express your continued interest in the opportunity. By following up after the interview, you not only show your professionalism and dedication but also stand out as a proactive candidate who is genuinely interested in the position.

**Follow-Up Email Example**

*Subject: Thank You for the Interview Opportunity*

*Dear [Interviewer's Name],*

*I would like to extend my sincere gratitude for the opportunity to interview for the [Position Name] at [Company Name]. I thoroughly enjoyed our conversation and learning more about the exciting work being done at your organization.*

*I am particularly excited about the prospect of contributing my [specific skill/experience discussed] to the [specific project/team* discussed] that we discussed during the interview. I am confident that my background aligns well with the requirements of the role, and I am eager to bring my expertise to your team.

Thank you once again for considering my application. I look forward to the possibility of working together and contributing to the continued success of [Company Name].

Warm regards,

[Your Name]

[Your Contact Information]

### Follow-Up Call Example

[After a day or two from the interview]

You: Hello [Interviewer's Name], I hope you're doing well. I wanted to express my gratitude for the opportunity to interview for the [Position Name]. I thoroughly enjoyed our conversation, and I wanted to follow up to reiterate my interest in the role and inquire about any updates on the hiring timeline.

Interviewer: Thank you for reaching out, [Your Name]. I appreciate your continued interest in the position. We are currently in the process of reviewing candidates and should have a decision within the next week. Is there anything else you would like to share or any additional information I can provide you with at this time?

You: Thank you for the update, [Interviewer's Name]. I am excited about the prospect of potentially joining your team and am available for any further discussions or interviews if needed. Please feel free to reach out if there are any additional details required from my end.

*Interviewer: Thank you for your proactive approach. We will be in touch with any updates.*

*You: Great, thank you for your time. I appreciate the opportunity and look forward to potentially working together. Have a great day.*

*Interviewer: You're welcome. Have a good day as well.*

Remember to speak confidently and professionally and express your interest in the role throughout the call. This script can serve as a guide, but feel free to personalize it based on your interview experience and relationship with the interviewer.

## 97. USE REJECTION TO YOUR ADVANTAGE

When you receive a job rejection email, it can be disheartening, but it's essential to respond in a composed and professional manner (Boogard, 2025). Take a moment to express your gratitude for the opportunity to interview for the position. Showing appreciation for the time and consideration of the hiring team demonstrates your professionalism and leaves a positive impression.

Additionally, don't hesitate to ask for feedback on why you weren't selected for the role. This feedback can be invaluable in identifying areas where you can improve, whether it's enhancing your skills, fine-tuning your interview responses, or addressing any potential weaknesses. By seeking constructive criticism, you demonstrate a proactive approach to self-improvement and show that you are open to learning from each experience.

Similarly, when faced with an unsuccessful interview, view it as a learning opportunity rather than a setback. Take the time to reflect on the interview process. Consider what went well and where there is room for improvement. Identify any moments during the interview where you may have faltered or areas where you could have provided stronger responses. Use this self-reflection to assess your strengths and weaknesses, allowing you to refine your approach for future interviews.

Remember, each interview experience, even if unsuccessful, provides valuable insights that can help you grow and develop as a candidate. Embrace the feedback, learn from your experiences, and continue to refine your skills and interview techniques. By adopting a positive and growth-oriented mindset, you can transform rejection into a stepping stone towards achieving your career goals.

## 98. SEEK CONSTRUCTIVE FEEDBACK POST-INTERVIEW

Seeking constructive feedback after an interview is an essential step, and it holds significance regardless of whether you receive a job offer or not (*How to Ask for Feedback After an Interview*, 2024). By requesting feedback, you demonstrate a proactive approach to self-improvement and a genuine interest in gaining insights into your performance. This feedback can help you understand the areas where you excelled and where you may need to focus on improvement, such as your communication style, presentation of skills and experiences, or overall impression you made. It can also provide valuable information about how your qualifications and experiences align with the employer's needs and expectations.

Seek feedback from the interviewers themselves, if possible, as they can offer direct, specific insights into your performance. Additionally, consider reaching out to trusted mentors, colleagues, or even friends for their perspectives. Sometimes, an outside viewpoint can offer a different perspective on your interview performance. When receiving feedback, approach it with an open mind and focus on identifying areas for growth and development rather than dwelling on any perceived shortcomings. Utilize the feedback to refine your interview techniques, enhance your responses to common interview questions, and polish your overall presentation for future opportunities.

## 99. BUILD RESILIENCE

Focusing on building resilience and staying motivated is key to navigating the ups and downs of the job search process (System One, 2023). Building resilience involves developing the ability to bounce back from challenges, setbacks, and rejections. It's important to understand that not every interview will result in an offer, and that's okay. Each experience provides an opportunity for personal and professional growth. Stay motivated by setting clear, achievable goals for yourself, whether it's researching the company thoroughly, practicing common interview questions, or refining your elevator pitch.

Visualizing success can also be a powerful motivator. Take a moment to imagine yourself acing the interview, confidently showcasing your skills and expertise. This positive visualization can boost your confidence and help you approach the interview with a can-do attitude. When faced with obstacles or moments of self-doubt, remember to practice self-care strategies. Engage in activities that relax and rejuvenate you, such as meditation, exercise, or spending time with loved ones.

Seek support from friends, family, or a mentor who can provide encouragement and perspective. Remember to celebrate your achievements and strengths, no matter how small they may seem. By cultivating resilience and staying motivated, you can navigate the interview process with grace and confidence, demonstrating your ability to adapt to challenges and showcasing a determined, positive attitude that will impress potential employers.

## 100. OPTIMIZE YOUR JOB SEARCH

Optimizing your job search is a critical step in securing the right opportunities that align with your career goals (*11 Types of Job-Hunting Strategies*, n.d.). Start by refining your application materials, including your résumé and cover letter. Tailor these documents to highlight your relevant skills, experiences, and accomplishments that directly relate to the job you are applying for. Customizing your application materials will demonstrate to potential employers that you have taken the time to understand their needs and can meet them effectively.

In addition to tailoring your application, consider leveraging various job search resources to expand your reach. Utilize online job boards, such as LinkedIn, Indeed, or industry-specific websites, to uncover a wide range of job opportunities. Networking platforms can also be valuable tools for connecting with industry professionals, attending virtual job fairs, and identifying potential leads. Make use of your professional connections, including former colleagues, mentors, and friends, to tap into hidden job opportunities and receive referrals.

To stay proactive in your job search, set up job alerts and notifications to receive real-time updates on new job postings in your desired field. This will allow you to stay ahead of the competition and submit your applications promptly. As you prepare for your interview, research the company thoroughly to understand its values, culture, and recent developments. This knowledge will not only help you tailor your responses during the interview but also demonstrate your genuine interest in the organization.

Lastly, practice your interview skills by preparing responses to common interview questions, highlighting your strengths, and addressing any potential weaknesses. Develop a list of insightful questions to ask the interviewer, showcasing your curiosity and engagement with the company. By optimizing your job search strategy, you can effectively position yourself as a strong candidate, increase your chances of landing interviews, and ultimately secure the right job that aligns with your career aspirations.

## 101. STAY MOTIVATED DURING YOUR JOB SEARCH

As you navigate the daunting journey of job searching, it's crucial to prioritize staying motivated to maintain your drive and focus throughout the process (Lowe-MacAuley, 2023b). One effective strategy is to set specific, achievable goals for yourself. This could involve creating a daily or weekly task list that includes activities such as researching companies, customizing your résumé and cover letter for each application, networking with industry professionals, or practicing your interview skills. By breaking down your job search into manageable steps, you can track your progress and maintain a sense of accomplishment along the way.

In addition to setting goals, celebrate even the smallest victories during your job search. Whether it's receiving a callback for an interview, receiving positive feedback on your résumé, or making a meaningful new connection, take the time to acknowledge and appreciate these achievements. Recognizing your progress and efforts can help boost your confidence and motivation to continue pursuing your job search with enthusiasm.

Building a support system can also be instrumental in staying motivated during your job search. Lean on friends, family, or mentors who can provide encouragement, advice, and a listening ear when needed. Surrounding yourself with positive influences can help you stay motivated, combat self-doubt, and maintain a sense of perspective throughout the ups and downs of the job search process.

Furthermore, remember that facing rejection or setbacks is a normal part of the job search journey. Each experience can provide valuable lessons and opportunities for growth. Instead of viewing rejections as failures, see them as stepping stones toward finding the right opportunity that aligns with your skills and aspirations. Keep a positive mindset, focus on your strengths, and learn from each experience to become a stronger and more resilient job seeker.

As we approach the conclusion of this book, it's evident that mastering the art of negotiation and closing with confidence stand as pivotal milestones in the interview process. Let's break down these key insights and explore how to leverage them for career advancement:

### *Art of Negotiation*

- Understand the Dynamics of Negotiation: It's essential to recognize that negotiation is not just about salary but also about benefits, work-life balance, career advancement opportunities, and more.
- Develop Effective Communication Skills: Learning how to articulate your value, actively listen to the other party's perspective, and communicate your requirements clearly is pivotal in successful negotiations.
- Create Win-Win Situations: Striving for outcomes where both parties feel satisfied and valued can foster long-term professional relationships.

### *Closing With Confidence*

- Demonstrate Your Enthusiasm: Expressing genuine interest in the role and the company during the closing stages of an interview can leave a positive impression on the interviewer.
- Showcase Value and Fit: Summarizing how your skills, experiences, and qualities align with the company's needs and culture can reinforce the interviewer's confidence in your candidacy.

- Ask Pertinent Questions: Concluding the interview with well-thought-out queries about the role, team dynamics, or company vision demonstrates your engagement and foresight.

## *Learnings for Career Advancement*

- Securing the Job Offer: Applying the strategies of negotiation and confident closing can enhance your chances of receiving a favorable job offer, including desirable compensation and benefits.
- Thrive in Professional Journey: The skills acquired through mastering negotiation and confident closing are valuable beyond just interviews. They prepare you to navigate professional challenges, advocate for yourself, and foster productive working relationships.
- Professional Growth: Engaging in effective negotiation and confident closing also builds your professional reputation as assertive, strategic, and collaborative—qualities that are highly valued in the workplace.
- Personal Development: The process of mastering negotiation and confident closing can also contribute to your personal growth, boosting your self-confidence and assertiveness.

# CONCLUSION

 *Don't watch the clock; do what it does. Keep going.*

— SAM LEVENSON

As we reach the conclusion of this book, I want to tip my hat to you for embarking on this journey of self-improvement and growth. It's been an incredible ride, and I truly believe that you're now better equipped to tackle any interview with confidence and skill.

The essence of this book is to empower you to embrace your unique strengths, refine your storytelling abilities, and excel in captivating interviewers. Beyond providing practical strategies for interview success, it serves as a source of inspiration and encouragement for you as you navigate feelings of anxiety, uncertainty, and apprehension when faced with the daunting prospect of interacting with an interview panel.

It's important to recognize that the challenges and fears associated with interviews are universal and shared by many individuals on their professional journeys. The book serves as a beacon of reassurance, reminding you that you are not alone in your pursuit of career advancement and personal growth. By imparting 101 transformative insights and perspectives on approaching interviews differently, it equips you with the confidence and tools needed to navigate the interview process with authenticity and resilience.

One key takeaway from the book is the realization that an interview is more than a mere evaluation of qualifications; it is an opportunity for you to communicate your genuine self, aspirations, and potential for making a meaningful contribution. By internalizing this perspective, you are encouraged to go beyond conventional interview norms and focus on articulating your unique value proposition, passion, and vision for the future. Through the process of self-discovery and introspection advocated in the book, you can align your professional objectives with your personal values, fostering a deep sense of purpose and authenticity in your interactions with interviewers.

The key takeaway from this journey is simple: You are a force to be reckoned with, armed with a unique set of skills, experiences, and qualities that make you one-of-a-kind. Embrace who you are, stand tall in your abilities, and let your light shine. You have the power to make a lasting impression and land the job of your dreams.

As we wrap up, I want to leave you with a story of triumph— a tale of someone who, like you, experienced the nervous jitters before an interview but emerged victorious. Imagine the exhilaration of that moment—the joy, the sense of accomplishment, and the exhilarating feeling of knowing that all your hard work has paid off. That could be your story. You have all the tools you need within you to create your own success narrative.

So, what's next for you? How about taking that first step, armed with your newfound knowledge and confidence, toward acing your next interview? Your dream job could be just an interview away, and you're more than ready to make it your own.

Lastly, if this book has empowered you, resonated with you, and guided you through the maze of interviews, I'd be honored if you could share your experience with others. Your review can be a light of hope for someone else who, like you, is on the path to career fulfillment.

Thank you for allowing me to be a part of your journey. I believe in you, and I can't wait to hear about your next triumph. Here's to you! Keep shining, keep believing, and keep conquering those interviews.

# REFERENCES

*Answering behavioural-based interview questions.* (2024). Indeed Career Guide. https://uk.indeed.com/career-advice/interviewing/resilience-inter view-questions

Augustine, A. (2021, July 8). *Just Be Yourself: How to Sound Authentic in an Interview.* TopInterview. https://topinterview.com/interview-advice/ sound-authentic-in-job-interview

Barraza, S. (2023, November 10). *Zoom to Success: Insider Tips for Nailing Your TV Interview.* Aker Ink. https://akerink.com/zoom-to-success-insider-tips-for-nailing-your-tv-interview/

Beisler, C. (2015, March 23). *What Hiring Managers Wish Job Seekers Already Knew.* BridgeView. https://www.bridgeviewit.com/blog/hiring-managers-wish-job-seekers-already-knew/

Boogaard, K. (2024, May 14). *The STAR Method: The secret to acing your next job interview.* The Muse. https://www.themuse.com/advice/star-inter view-method

Chan, G. (n.d.). *50 Empowering Personal Branding Quotes For Your Journey.* Forbes. https://www.forbes.com/sites/goldiechan/2024/01/03/50-empowering-personal-branding-quotes-for-your-journey/

Chan, S. (2024, August 19). *How Early Should You Join a Zoom Interview?* Tactiq.io. https://tactiq.io/learn/how-early-should-you-join-a-zoom-interview

Cherry, K. (2024, April 1). *11 Signs of Low Self-Esteem.* Verywell Mind. https://www.verywellmind.com/signs-of-low-self-esteem-5185978

Clear, J. (2013). *Goal Setting: A Scientific Guide to Setting and Achieving Goals.* James Clear. https://jamesclear.com/goal-setting

Clinic, C. (2019, May). *What to Eat When You Have a Job Interview.* Cleveland Clinic. https://health.clevelandclinic.org/what-to-eat-when-you-have-a-job-interview

Collins, L. (2022, October 27). *5 Pre-Interview Workout Routines.* Vault. https://vault.com/blogs/interviewing/pre-interview-workout-routines

*Conduct a Mock Interview Online in 5 Steps.* (2024). Indeed Career Guide. https://www.indeed.com/career-advice/interviewing/mock-interview-online

Cronkleton, E. (2019, April 9). *10 Breathing Techniques.* Healthline. https://www.healthline.com/health/breathing-exercise

Cuncic, A. (2024, February 12). *7 Active Listening Techniques for Better Communication.* Verywell Mind. https://www.verywellmind.com/what-is-active-listening-3024343

*The Dangers of Oversharing in a Job Interview.* (2023, December 19). Back to Work Connect. https://backtoworkconnect.ie/careerhub/the-dangers-of-oversharing-in-a-job-interview/

D'Souza, J. (2024, December 24). *Online Interview Statistics by Application, Software, Time, Gender, Market Share and Challenges.* Coolest Gadgets. https://www.coolest-gadgets.com/online-interview-statistics/

*Developing Your Elevator Pitch.* (n.d.). Center for Career Development. https://careerdevelopment.princeton.edu/guides/networking/developing-your-elevator-pitch

Dweck, C. (2015, March 2). *Carol Dweck: A Summary of The Two Mindsets.* Farnam Street. https://fs.blog/carol-dweck-mindset/

Editorial Team, I. (2023, February 4). *10 Tips for Maintaining a Positive Attitude.* Indeed Career Guide. https://www.indeed.com/career-advice/career-development/how-to-keep-a-positive-attitude

*11 Types of Job-Hunting Strategies (With Tips).* (n.d.). Indeed Career Guide. https://www.indeed.com/career-advice/finding-a-job/job-hunting

*8 surprising statistics about interviews.* (n.d.). Twin Employment. https://www.twinemployment.com/uk/blog/8-surprising-statistics-about-interviews/

*Ensure a successful virtual interview by mastering time zone scheduling.* (2024, October 11). LinkedIn. https://www.linkedin.com/advice/0/youre-navigating-time-zone-disparities-virtual-a81me

*Filler Words: Definition, Examples and How to Avoid Them.* (n.d.). Indeed Career Guide. https://www.indeed.com/career-advice/career-development/filler-word

Franklin, B. (2019). *Forbes Quotes Thoughts on the Business of Life.* Forbes. https://www.forbes.com/quotes/1107/

Gillett, R. (2015, June 22). *Tricks to instantly appear trustworthy.* Business Insider. https://www.businessinsider.com/tricks-to-instantly-appear-trustworthy-2015-6

Glide Outplacement. (2016, August 16). *Bad night's sleep before a job interview.* Glide Outplacement. https://www.outplacement.net.au/blog/bad-nights-sleep-before-job-interview/

Goldman, R. (2022, November 4). *Affirmations: What They Are and How to Use*

*Them.* EverydayHealth. https://www.everydayhealth.com/emotional-health/what-are-affirmations/

Guest. (2016, June 14). *8 Steps to Your Pre-Interview Social Media Clean Up.* Undercover Recruiter. https://theundercoverrecruiter.com/social-media-clean-interview/

Hailey, L. (2022, April 22). *9 Simple Tips to Smile Better (in any situation!).* Science of People. https://www.scienceofpeople.com/smile/

Hcareers. (2025). Hcareers. https://www.hcareers.com/article/career-advice/5-statements-that-will-convince-an-employer-to-hire-you

Heller, G. (2023, February 15). *When preparing for a job interview, it is essential to tailor your responses to the specific company and audience.* LinkedIn. https://www.linkedin.com/pulse/tailor-your-job-interview-responses-specific-company-audience-heller/

Herrity, J. (2023, February 2). *15 Top Qualities Employers Look For in Job Candidates.* Indeed Career Guide. https://www.indeed.com/career-advice/finding-a-job/qualities-employers-want

*The hiring process explained in 15 steps.* Manatal Resources. (n.d.). Www.manatal.com. https://www.manatal.com/glossary/hiring-process

*Highlight Your Achievements.* (2025). HEC Montréal. https://www.hec.ca/en/students/support-resources/career-management/career-development-path/showcase-yourself/highlight-your-achievements/highlight-your-achievements.html

*Honesty in Interviews: Keeping a Balance.* (2025). Gradsingapore. https://gradsingapore.com/graduate-careers-advice/interview-tips-and-techniques/honesty-in-interviews-keeping-a-balance

*How to Ace Your Virtual Interview.* (2024). Indeed Career Guide. https://www.indeed.com/career-advice/interviewing/what-to-wear-for-a-zoom-interview

*How to Ask for Feedback After an Interview (2024 Guide).* (2024). Indeed Career Guide. https://au.indeed.com/career-advice/interviewing/how-to-ask-for-feedback-after-interview

How to Conduct the Mock Interview (n.d.). OCT Training and Resources. https://octresources.stanford.edu/mock-interviews/how-conduct-mock-interview

*How to Create a Virtual Interview Cheat Sheet.* (2024, January 21). Industry Connect. https://mckelveyconnect.washu.edu/blog/2024/01/21/how-to-create-a-virtual-interview-cheat-sheet/

*How to Explain Employment Gaps in an Interview.* (n.d.). Indeed Career Guide.

https://www.indeed.com/career-advice/interviewing/how-to-explain-employment-gaps

*How to Research a Company for a Job Interview.* (2021, September 21). Purdue Global. https://www.purdueglobal.edu/blog/careers/research-company-job-interview/

*How to sit during an interview.* (n.d.). Korn Ferry. https://www.kornferry.com/insights/featured-topics/career-advice/how-to-sit-in-an-interview-2

*How to Stop Rambling in Job Interviews.* (2016, July 20). The Muse. https://www.themuse.com/advice/5-strategies-thatll-stop-you-from-rambling-your-way-through-an-interview

*How to Test Your Tech for a Video Interview.* (2024). Indeed. https://www.indeed.com/hire/c/info/how-to-test-tech-for-video-interview

*How to Write a Punchy Personal Story.* (n.d.). Ship30for30. https://www.ship30for30.com/post/how-to-write-a-punchy-personal-story

*23 Most Interesting First Impression Statistics to Know.* (2024, June 30). Passive Secrets. https://passivesecrets.com/first-impression-statistics/

Indeed Editorial Team. (2023, May 11). Top 16 Common Job Interview Questions and Answers. Indeed. https://www.indeed.com/career-advice/interviewing/top-interview-questions-and-answers

Jezra. (2020, March 26). *How to Connect on Video Interviews.* Speak up for Success. https://speakupforsuccess.com/connect-on-video-interviews/

*The Job Interview Thank You Email Template You Need.* (n.d.). The Muse. https://www.themuse.com/advice/how-to-write-an-interview-thankyou-note-an-email-template

Jobsite.co.uk. (2013, April 2). *5 Ways to Use Positive Language in an Interview.* YouTube. https://www.youtube.com/watch?v=snLI53KdgR0

Lipschutz, N. (2022, January 17). *How do I make my speech more relatable?* Natsuyo Lipschutz. Natsuyo Lipschutz. https://natsuyolipschutz.us/how-do-i-make-my-speech-more-relatable

Lowe-MacAuley, K. (2023a, April 11). *Salary Negotiation: How to Find a Job's Fair Market Value.* FlexJobs. https://www.flexjobs.com/blog/post/how-to-research-the-fair-market-value-of-a-job

Lowe-MacAuley, K. (2023b, April 26). *How to Stay Motivated During a Frustrating Job Search.* FlexJobs. https://www.flexjobs.com/blog/post/maintain-positive-attitude-frustrating-job-search

Madell, R. (2021). *How to Respond to Pushback During Salary Negotiation.* FlexJobs. https://doi.org/10/16154148/How-to-Respond-to-Pushback-During-Salary-Negotiation-2

Magazine, B. (2022, December 19). *7 Things To Do If Your Salary Negotiation Fails.* Brainz Magazine. https://www.brainzmagazine.com/post/7-things-to-do-if-your-salary-negotiation-fails

*Mastering the Art of Storytelling: How Jobseekers Can Captivate Hiring Teams.* (2024, May 29). InterviewFocus. https://interviewfocus.com/mastering-the-art-of-storytelling-how-jobseekers-can-captivate-hiring-teams/

Mayo Clinic Staff. (2023, November 21). *Positive thinking: Stop negative self-talk to reduce stress.* Mayo Clinic. https://www.mayoclinic.org/healthy-lifestyle/stress-management/in-depth/positive-thinking/art-20043950

Mays, A. D. (2025). *Blocked.* LinkedIn. https://www.linkedin.com/pulse/job-descriptions-how-read-them-like-pro-anthony-d-mays/

McKee, P. (2015, November 5). *Can You Do the Digital Handshake?* Career Confidential. https://careerconfidential.com/digital-handshake/

Miles, M. (2023, May 2). *Power Poses: 6 Examples to Unleash Your Inner Confidence.* BetterUp. https://www.betterup.com/blog/power-poses

*Most Powerful Things To Say in a Job Interview + Examples.* (2025). Indeed Career Guide. https://www.indeed.com/career-advice/interviewing/interview-vocabulary

Nicholls, S. (2015, April 2). *Is Your Voice Sabotaging Your Job Interview?* Executive Connexions. https://www.executiveconnexions.com/articles/interview-skills/is-the-sound-of-your-voice-sabotaging-your-job-interview/

Overvest, M. (2022, November 1). *Salary Negotiation Statistics 2023 — 18 Key Figures.* Procurement Tactics. https://procurementtactics.com/salary-negotiation-statistics/

Pelta, R. (2022, March 2). *Video Interview Background Tips: What to Include and More.* FlexJobs. https://www.flexjobs.com/blog/post/video-interview-background-really-says

McConnell, J. (2018, July 31). *I Was Rejected For Fidgeting In Interviews But These 5 Body Language Hacks Changed Everything.* Cheeky Scientist. https://cheekyscientist.com/rejected-in-interviews-but-body-language-changed-everything/

*Phone Interviews vs. In-Person Interviews (Pros and Cons).* (n.d.). Indeed Career Guide. https://www.indeed.com/career-advice/interviewing/phone-interview-vs-in-person

*The Power of Hand Gestures During Interviews.* (n.d.). Social-Hire. https://social-hire.com/blog/candidate/the-power-of-hand-gestures-during-interviews

Prichard, M. (2017, March 16). *Answer Tough Interview Questions By Perfecting the Pivot.* Mac's List. https://www.macslist.org/interviews/answer-tough-interview-questions-perfecting-pivot

*Reading the Room Gives You an Edge — No Matter Who You're Talking To.* (n.d.). BetterUp. https://www.betterup.com/blog/reading-the-room

*Self-talk.* (2019, November 10). Healthdirect Australia. https://www.healthdirect.gov.au/self-talk

Semuels, A. (2023, June 14). *You're Not Imagining It—Job Hunting is Getting Worse.* Time. https://time.com/6287012/why-finding-job-is-difficult/

*7 Ways How To Identify Your Personal Strengths.* (2021, July 29). HIGH5 TEST. https://high5test.com/identifying-personal-strengths/

*Silence is Golden: Mute Etiquette for Video Calls to Minimize Distractions.* 21st Century AV. (2023, May 14). https://21stcenturyav.com/video-call-mute-etiquette/

*Six Steps to Give a Great Handshake.* (2017, October 2). Science of People. https://www.scienceofpeople.com/handshake/

*60 Inspirational Quotes for a New Job.* (n.d.). Indeed Career Guide. https://www.indeed.com/career-advice/starting-new-job/quote-for-new-job

*62 Words of Encouragement for a Job Interview.* (n.d.). Indeed Career Guide. https://www.indeed.com/career-advice/interviewing/words-of-encouragement-for-job-interview

*The Smart Email to Send When You Get Rejected for a Job.* (2017, June 19). The Muse. https://www.themuse.com/advice/this-is-the-email-smart-people-send-when-theyre-rejected-for-a-job

Somanathan, S. (2024, November 11). *How to Follow Up After an Interview: Do's, Don'ts & Examples.* ClickUp. https://clickup.com/blog/how-to-follow-up-after-an-interview/

System One. (2023, November 6). *10 Tips to Stay Motivated During a Long Job Search.* System One. https://systemone.com/blog/10-tips-to-stay-motivated-during-a-long-job-search/

*10 Closing Statements to Use After an Interview.* (n.d.). Indeed Career Guide. https://www.indeed.com/career-advice/interviewing/closing-statements-in-an-interview

*10 Ways to Build a Rapport With Your Interviewer.* (n.d.). Hays. https://www.hays.co.jp/en/10-ways-to-build-a-rapport-with-your-interviewer

*10 Ways to Find the Name of a Hiring Manager (With Examples).* (2025). Indeed Career Guide. https://www.indeed.com/career-advice/finding-a-job/how-to-find-hiring-manager

The Muse Editor. (2013, October 15). *51 Great Questions to Ask in an Interview.* The Muse. https://www.themuse.com/advice/51-interview-questions-you-should-be-asking

The Muse Editor. (2014, October 15). *How to Write a Cover Letter: The All-Time Best Tips.* The Muse. https://www.themuse.com/advice/how-to-write-a-cover-letter-31-tips-you-need-to-know

theK. (2013, March 6). *Lighting Tips for Remote Video Interview.* GMAT Club Forums. https://gmatclub.com/forum/lighting-tips-for-remote-video-interview-148816.html

*12 Quick Mini-Meditations to Calm Your Mind and Body.* (2017). Psychology Today. https://www.psychologytoday.com/intl/blog/changepower/201703/12-quick-mini-meditations-calm-your-mind-and-body

*In This Tight Labor Market, Employers Still Have Candidate Deal-Breakers.* (2018, August 24). CareerBuilder. https://resources.careerbuilder.com/news-research/in-this-tight-labor-market-employers-still-have-candidate-deal-breakers

*Tips for Choosing the Best Job References.* (2024). Indeed Career Guide. https://www.indeed.com/career-advice/resumes-cover-letters/choosing-best-job-references

*The Ultimate Salary Negotiation Script For Every Scenario.* (2024). Faircomp. https://www.faircomp.io/resources/the-ultimate-salary-negotiation-script-for-every-scenario

University at Buffalo. (2024). Socialwork.buffalo.edu. https://socialwork.buffalo.edu/resources/self-care-starter-kit/additional-self-care-resources/developing-your-support-system.html

University of Colorado. (2014, December 16). *25 Quick Ways to Reduce Stress.* Colorado Law. https://www.colorado.edu/law/25-quick-ways-reduce-stress

Walsh, H. (2023, February 19). *Planning your journey to interview.* MARS Recruitment. https://www.marsrecruitment.co.uk/planning-your-journey-to-interview-2/

Warley, S. (n.d.). *Find Your Why to Get Unstuck.* Life Skills That Matter. https://www.lifeskillsthatmatter.com/blog/find-your-why

*What do you do if your virtual interviewee has technical difficulties?* (2024). LinkedIn. https://www.linkedin.com/advice/0/what-do-you-your-virtual-interviewee-has-technical-g2lae

*What Is Making Eye Contact?* (n.d.). Indeed Career Guide. https://www.indeed.com/career-advice/interviewing/making-eye-contact

*What to Wear to an Interview: 2022 Guide.* (n.d.). Coursera. https://www.coursera.org/articles/what-to-wear-to-an-interview

Yasmina. (2024, September 5). *The most effective negotiation techniques.*

Beyond by Esade. https://www.esade.edu/beyond/en/effective-negotiation-techniques/

*You're in the middle of a crucial interview. How do you navigate an unexpected phone call interruption?* (2024). LinkedIn. https://www.linkedin.com/advice/3/youre-middle-crucial-interview-how-do-you-navigate-gsv8f

Zimmer, J. (2019, November 12). *Pauses in a speech: Why, when and how.* Manner of Speaking. https://mannerofspeaking.org/2019/11/12/pauses-in-a-speech-why-when-and-how/

Zucker, R. (2022, June 7). *10 Red Flags to Watch Out for in a Job Interview.* Harvard Business Review. https://hbr.org/2022/06/10-red-flags-to-watch-out-for-in-a-job-interview

www.ingramcontent.com/pod-product-compliance
Lightning Source LLC
Chambersburg PA
CBHW021154130626
46554CB00005B/1812